U.S. Policy Toward Northeastern Europe

Report of an Independent Task Force
Sponsored by the
Council on Foreign Relations

Zbigniew Brzezinski, Chairman
F. Stephen Larrabee, Project Director

The Council on Foreign Relations, Inc., a nonprofit, nonpartisan national membership organization founded in 1921, is dedicated to promoting understanding of international affairs through the free and civil exchange of ideas. The Council's members are dedicated to the belief that America's peace and prosperity are firmly linked to that of the world. From this flows the mission of the Council: to foster America's understanding of its fellow members of the international community, near and far, their peoples, cultures, histories, hopes, quarrels, and ambitions; and thus to serve, protect, and advance America's own global interests through study and debate, private and public.

THE COUNCIL TAKES NO INSTITUTIONAL POSITION ON POLICY ISSUES AND HAS NO AFFILIATION WITH THE U.S. GOVERNMENT. ALL STATEMENTS OF FACT AND EXPRESSIONS OF OPINION CONTAINED IN ALL ITS PUBLICATIONS ARE THE SOLE RESPONSIBILITY OF THE AUTHOR OR AUTHORS.

The Council on Foreign Relations will sponsor an Independent Task Force when (1) an issue of current and critical importance to U.S. foreign policy arises, and (2) it seems that a group diverse in backgrounds and perspectives may, nonetheless, be able to reach a meaningful consensus on a policy through private and nonpartisan deliberations. Typically, a Task Force meets between two and five times over a brief period to ensure the relevance of its work.

Upon reaching a conclusion, a Task Force issues a report, and the Council publishes its text and posts it on the Council website. Task Force Reports can take three forms: (1) a strong and meaningful policy consensus, with Task Force members endorsing the general policy thrust and judgments reached by the group, though not necessarily every finding and recommendation; (2) a report stating the various policy positions, each as sharply and fairly as possible; or (3) a "Chairman's Report," where Task Force members who agree with the Chairman's Report may associate themselves with it, while those who disagree may submit dissenting statements. Upon reaching a conclusion, a Task Force may also ask individuals who were not members of the Task Force to associate themselves with the Task Force Report to enhance its impact. All Task Force Reports "benchmark" their findings against current administration policy in order to make explicit areas of agreement and disagreement. The Task Force is solely responsible for its report. The Council takes no institutional position.

For further information about the Council or this Task Force, please write the Council on Foreign Relations, 58 East 68th Street, New York, NY 10021, or call the Director of Communications at (212) 434-9400. Visit our website at *www.foreignrelations.org*.

CONTENTS

FOREWORD

During the Cold War, northeastern Europe was a strategic back-water and received relatively little attention in U.S. policy. Since the end of the Cold War, however, the region has become a focal point of U.S. policy. The Clinton administration has given north-eastern Europe high priority and viewed the region as a labora-tory for promoting closer regional cooperation and reknitting Europe—both eastern and western—into a more cohesive eco-nomic and political unit. Administration policy has also been designed to reach out to Russia and to include Russia in region-al cooperation arrangements in northeastern Europe.

Recognizing all this, the Council on Foreign Relations spon-sored an Independent Task Force on U.S. Policy Toward North-eastern Europe to examine the challenges confronting the United States in northeastern Europe and to recommend a policy to advance U.S. interests in the region. Zbigniew Brzezinski, former national security adviser to President Jimmy Carter and respected author and strategic thinker, chaired the Task Force. F. Stephen Larrabee, a former National Security Council staff member and leading European-affairs expert currently at the RAND Corpo-ration in Washington, D.C., was the project director. I would also like to note that the Task Force was originally conceived of and proposed by Paula J. Dobriansky, vice president and director of the Council's Washington program.

The Task Force members endorse the general thrust of the admin-istration's policy, especially its emphasis on enhancing regional coop-eration in northeastern Europe and encouraging Russian participation in regional cooperative efforts. At the same time, the report rec-ommends that a number of steps be taken to enhance the viabil-ity and effectiveness of the administration's policy. In particular, the administration should differentiate among the Baltic states based on their performance and should admit them into Euro-Atlantic institutions individually rather than as a group. The Task Force also recommends that the next round of NATO enlargement include one Baltic state, provided that the state demonstrates the ability to meet the responsibilities of membership. However, the issue of Baltic membership should not be the exclusive or central focus of U.S. strategy toward northeastern Europe. Rather, the focus should be a broader and multifaceted policy to enhance regional cooperation and stability. Finally, the Task Force believes that if its strategy is to succeed, the administration needs to develop stronger support for its policy, both within Congress and among America's European allies, and devote more resources to implementing it.

Leslie H. Gelb
President
Council on Foreign Relations

ACKNOWLEDGMENTS

The Task Force chairman and project director would like to thank the members of the Task Force for their helpful comments on various drafts of this report. We would also like to thank Leslie H. Gelb, president of the Council, who was instrumental in the creation of the Task Force, and Paula J. Dobriansky, vice president and director of the Council's Washington Program, and her staff for arranging the Task Force meetings. Special thanks go to Daniel Fata, assistant to the vice president and Washington director of the Council, who served as Task Force rapporteur, for his administrative, editorial, and research assistance.

We would also like to thank Daniel Rose and David Hale for sharing their ideas with us and for commenting on the report. Finally, we would like to thank the Smith Richardson Foundation and the Arthur Ross Foundation for their generous support of the Task Force.

EXECUTIVE SUMMARY

INTRODUCTION

The Independent Task Force on U.S. Policy Toward Northeastern Europe sponsored by the Council on Foreign Relations was formed to examine the policy challenges confronting the United States in northeastern Europe and recommend measures to advance U.S. interests in the region.[1] The Task Force felt that northeastern Europe deserves special attention for several reasons.

First, during the Cold War, northeastern Europe was a strategic backwater and received relatively little attention in U.S. policy. However, since the end of the Cold War, the region has become an important focal point of U.S. policy. The Clinton administration has given northeastern Europe high priority and viewed the region as a laboratory for promoting closer regional cooperation and reknitting Europe—both eastern and western—into a more cohesive economic and political unit. As Secretary of State Madeleine Albright noted in her speech in Vilnius, Lithuania, in July 1997, "Our challenge is to build a fully integrated Europe that includes every European democracy willing to meet its responsibilities. That goal embraces the Baltic nations." Thus, to some extent, northeastern Europe can be seen as a test case for the Clinton administration's general approach toward post–Cold War Europe.

Second, northeastern Europe is also a test case for the administration's policy toward Russia. One of the key elements of the administration's policy has been its effort to reach out to Russia and to include Russia in regional cooperation arrangements in northeastern Europe. This effort has been designed to integrate Russia gradually into a broader European framework as well as to defuse Russian concerns about the integration of the Baltic states into Euro-

---

[1] Northeastern Europe is defined as including the Baltic littoral states, especially the Baltic states and the Nordics, but also Poland and Germany as well as northwestern Russia (i.e., St. Petersburg, Murmansk, Novgorod, and Kaliningrad).

Atlantic institutions, especially NATO. This policy is seen by the administration as a litmus test of its effort to overcome the old zero-sum Cold War paradigm and demonstrate that greater regional cooperation can bring benefits to all, including Russia. Thus, how well this policy succeeds will have broader implications for the administration's policy toward Russia as a whole.

Third, three critical areas of U.S. policy interest—the Baltics, the Nordics, and Russia—intersect in northeastern Europe. Instability in the region would affect all three interests. Moreover, the Baltic region is the one region in Europe where a U.S.-Russian confrontation is still conceivable. Thus, the United States has a strong stake in defusing the potential for conflict in the region and promoting its stable economic and political development.

Fourth, the United States faces a number of critical challenges in the region. One of the most important is managing the security aspirations of the Baltic states. The Baltic states are tied to Europe historically and culturally. They share Western values and aspirations. Having thrown off the shackles of communism and Soviet domination, the Baltic states, like their counterparts in Central Europe, want to join Europe and Euro-Atlantic institutions. How the United States seeks to accommodate their security aspirations will be a major test of the U.S. commitment to creating a "Europe whole and free" and its ability to overcome the zero-sum logic of the Cold War.

Fifth, the policy challenges in northeastern Europe—particularly those in the Baltic subregion—directly touch on Russia's security interests and have important implications for U.S.-Russian relations. Top Russian officials have reiterated on numerous occasions that Baltic membership in NATO could have serious repercussions for Russia's relations with NATO and the newly established Russia-NATO Council in particular. Although such statements should not necessarily be taken at face value, they highlight the sensitivity of the Baltic issue among the Russian policy elite and ensure that it will remain a highly contentious issue in U.S. relations with Russia.

Sixth, the issue of security in northeastern Europe directly affects U.S. relations with the Nordic states, especially Sweden and

Finland: the Baltic states are in the Nordic states' strategic back-yard. Thus, how the Baltic issue is handled has direct implications for Nordic security—and especially for relations of the Nordic states with Russia. Neither Sweden nor Finland wants to see the Baltic or Nordic region become a gray zone or flash point. At the same time, neither wants to assume the primary responsibility for the security of the Baltic states, which would overburden the capability of either nation.

Finally, security issues in northeastern Europe pose important dilemmas for U.S. policy toward NATO. The Baltic issue is the trickiest and most sensitive part of the enlargement puzzle. The Clinton administration has committed itself to helping the Baltic states gain membership in NATO. But many senators have reservations about further enlargement, especially to the Baltic states. So do many of America's NATO allies. Thus, gaining support for Baltic membership could be difficult and will require the administration to build a consensus for its policy both in the U.S. Senate and within the alliance.

CURRENT POLICY AND PRIMARY RECOMMENDATIONS

The Clinton administration has given northeastern Europe a high priority and has sought to develop a coherent overall policy toward the region. The administration's policy has proceeded along three separate but closely related tracks.

The first track has been designed to integrate the Baltic states into Euro-Atlantic institutions and structures. This track has been regarded by the administration as a critical test of its ability to overcome the zero-sum logic of the Cold War and as a key element of its effort to enhance stability in Europe as a whole. It is also the most controversial and sensitive element of U.S. policy because of its potential impact on relations with Russia.

The second track of the administration's policy is designed to strengthen relations with the Nordic states and coordinate efforts to improve regional cooperation. It focuses on six major areas: law enforcement, the environment, energy, public health, strengthening civil courts, and business promotion. Cooperation with Sweden and Finland in particular has been strengthened. As a result of this close cooperation, relations with the Nordic countries are better today than at any time since the end of World War II.

The third track has been designed to encourage Russia's greater participation and involvement in regional cooperation. Particular attention has been focused on developing cooperation with northwestern Russia. The main vehicle for promoting this policy has been the Northern European Initiative (NEI), which aims to promote cross-border initiatives in areas such as trade and investment, institution building, energy management, infrastructure enhancement, nuclear-waste control, law enforcement, and the development of civil society.

The Task Force endorses the general thrust of the administration's policy, especially its emphasis on enhancing regional cooperation and encouraging Russian participation in regional cooperative efforts. It believes such efforts can contribute to enhancing regional stability and integrating Russia into a broader European framework over the long run. At the same time, the Task Force recommends that a number of steps be taken to enhance the viability and effectiveness of the administration's policy.

First, a senior-level State Department official should be appointed with specific responsibility for promoting regional cooperation in northeastern Europe and coordinating policy toward the region. He/she should report directly to the secretary of state. Unless this is done, there is a serious danger that many of the initiatives that have been launched will languish and/or lose bureaucratic momentum.

Second, the administration should put more resources behind its policy. The administration has laid out an ambitious agenda, but many of its goals are unlikely to be achieved unless they are followed up and sufficient resources are devoted to implementing them. In some areas—particularly regional cooperation between the Baltic states and Russia—there are already signs that momentum is beginning to flag. Many projects have not gotten off the ground because of lack of funds. Moreover, it will be difficult to get America's European allies, especially the Nordics, to do more unless the United States is willing to put more resources behind its vision.

Third, the United States should differentiate between the Baltic states based on their performance and should admit them into Euro-Atlantic institutions individually rather than as a group. This would recognize the growing differentiation that is taking place among the Baltic states. At the same time, it would provide an incentive for those not in the "fast lane" to improve their performance and qualifications for membership in these institutions.

Fourth, the next round of enlargement should include one Baltic state provided that state demonstrates the ability to meet the responsibilities of membership. Admitting one Baltic state in the next round would make clear that there are no "red lines" and complement the European Union's decision to put Estonia on a fast track for EU membership. Which Baltic state should be invited—and when—will depend on many factors, especially which state is best prepared to meet the responsibilities of membership at the time when NATO decides to enlarge again. At present, Lithuania has made the most progress in preparing for membership. It also has the best relationship with Russia and the smallest and best-integrated Russian minority. Its inclusion in NATO is thus likely to be the least problematic for Russia.

Fifth, the administration needs to do more to generate support for its policy in Congress. This is all the more important because the coalition in Congress that supported NATO enlargement in the first round could break up. Many moderate Democrats and moderate Republicans who supported the first round of enlargement are skeptical about the wisdom of an early second round and especially about including the Baltic states. Keeping the old enlargement coalition together will be difficult and will require sustained effort on the part of this administration or the next.

Sixth, the administration needs to develop greater support for its policy among America's NATO allies. Italy, France, Spain, Greece, and Turkey strongly support a "southern" opening in the next round of NATO enlargement. Germany, a key supporter of the inclusion of Central Europe in the first round of enlargement, is far less enthusiastic about the inclusion of the Baltic states. Thus, putting together a new allied coalition for including the Baltic states in NATO will require considerable diplomatic effort and skill on the administration's part.

However, the issue of Baltic membership in NATO needs to be prudently managed and be part of a broader, multifaceted strategy to enhance stability in northeastern Europe. *NATO membership should be an integral element of this strategy, but it should not be the exclusive or central focus of it.* As part of its effort to develop such a broader strategy, the United States should:

- *Use the Partnership for Peace (PFP) to increase interoperability and help prepare the Baltic states for NATO membership.* PFP provides an important mechanism for enhancing the ability of the Baltic states to operate more effectively with NATO and for helping them to prepare for NATO membership. The United States should increase the number of PFP exercises with the Baltic states as well as provide practical assistance of the kind extended to the three newest NATO members (Poland, Hungary, and the Czech Republic) after they received invitations.

- *Encourage the EU to put Latvia and Lithuania on the fast track to EU membership along with Estonia.* This could provide important reassurance to the Baltic states and act as an important deterrent to Russian pressure or intimidation. It would also relieve some of the pressure for membership in NATO. This, in turn, would reduce Russian anxieties and allow the NATO issue to be managed in a less intense atmosphere.

- *Enhance regional cooperation with Russia, including in the military field.* The more Russia is integrated into broader regional cooperation, the less nervous it is likely to be about Baltic membership in NATO over the long run. This is particularly true in the military field. PFP provides an important vehicle for engaging the Russians and for drawing them more closely into regional cooperation.

- *Encourage the Baltic states to integrate their Russian minorities more completely into Baltic political and social life.* The more the Russian minority is integrated into Baltic society, the less of a problem it is likely to be in each state and the less Russia will be able to exploit the minority issue for foreign policy purposes.

• *Encourage the Baltic states to address their past more forthrightly.* NATO is not just a military organization. It is also about values. As part of their effort to demonstrate their commitment to Western values, the Baltic countries need an honest reckoning with their past, including the Holocaust. They have taken the first step in this regard with the establishment of national historical commissions to deal with crimes committed under Nazi and totalitarian rule. However, these commissions need to be more than just formalities. They must address the crimes in a forthright and honest way. This would help to build bridges to various parts of the American political spectrum and would clearly demonstrate that these countries are committed to Western values.

• *Press the Baltic states to implement the Organization for Security and Cooperation in Europe (OSCE)–compliant legislation that was recently passed in Latvia and Estonia and increase funding to help them do it.* Although on paper the laws have been changed, many of the changes have not been fully implemented because of lack of resources. Increased U.S. funding to help the Baltic states provide language training for the Russian minority is particularly important and should be a top priority.

ADDITIONAL RECOMMENDATIONS

In addition, the Task Force makes the following specific recommendations:

Regional Cooperation
• Support for East European Democracy (SEED) money should be increased and refocused to emphasize social integration

and to promote regional cooperation programs with Russia. In addition, there needs to be more interaction and consultation between SEED officials dealing with Russia and those dealing with the Baltics.

- The United States should devote more resources to increasing regional cooperation between the Baltic states and Russia in priority areas: crime prevention, education, rule of law, environment, commerce, and energy.

- The United States should encourage greater regional cooperation in northeastern Europe, especially in cooperation with the EU. However, it should reject efforts to decouple Baltic and Nordic security from European security.

Baltic States
- The United States should use Title 8 money to fund more training and research on the Baltic region. A deeper and more thorough knowledge of the region can contribute to the development of more farsighted policies toward the area.

- The mission of the Baltic-American Enterprise Fund (BAEF) should be reoriented and focused more on helping to integrate the Russian minority into the social and political life of the Baltic countries. In particular, it should focus on supporting language training for teachers in the areas populated by the Russian minority.

- The United States should expand and diversify the American engagement in northeastern Europe and the Baltic areas. This engagement should extend beyond the federal government and should involve business, universities, nongovernmental organizations (NGOs), and even individual states. In particular, the U.S. government can capitalize on the interest of the states in the upper-midwest in fostering close cooperation with the Baltic region similar to the cooperation that has developed between the southeastern United States and Germany.

Europe/Nordics

- The United States should encourage the Nordic states to continue their assistance to and trade with the Baltic states, especially Latvia. The Nordics are the Baltic states' natural partners. Moreover, such assistance is likely to raise less suspicion in Moscow than if the United States plays a highly visible role.

- The United States should step up its cooperation with the EU in northeastern Europe. Finland's prime minister, Paavo Lipponen, has called for a "Northern Dimension" for the EU that is designed to promote regional cooperation with Russia in areas such as energy, infrastructure, and ecology. With Finland assuming the EU presidency in July 1999, this is the ideal time to work out an agreement on how the United States and the EU can cooperate more closely in northeastern Europe. In particular, the United States should work closely with Finland to promote closer EU-Russian-U.S. cooperation in northeastern Europe in areas such as drug-traffic control, energy development, and building civil society.

- The United States should encourage the European Union to accelerate the process of integrating the three Baltic states into the EU. This is particularly true in the case of Latvia, which has the largest Russian minority and whose economy is the most tightly connected with the Russian economy. If Latvia's performance continues to improve, the United States should encourage the EU to put Latvia on the fast track toward membership, along with Estonia. This would help anchor Latvia more firmly into Euro-Atlantic institutions and reduce its vulnerability. It would also provide a positive signal for Western investment in Latvia.

- Verbal encouragement and rhetoric must be matched by a willingness on the part of the United States to devote more resources to northeastern Europe. If the United States wants the EU to do more, it will have to do more itself. Otherwise the calls for the EU to allocate more resources to northeastern Europe are likely to have little effect.

Security and Defense

- The United States should encourage the Baltic countries to raise their defense spending to the level agreed to by the three newest members—Poland, Hungary, and the Czech Republic (2 percent of gross domestic product).

- The United States should increase foreign military financing (FMF) support to help the Baltic states implement the plans and priorities identified in the Defense Department study on the military capabilities of the Baltic states ("Kievenaar Study"). The Baltic states should be given preferential treatment because, unlike the other East European states, they had to create their militaries from scratch. This would require only a small increase in resources, but it could be very cost-effective.

- The United States should increase bilateral military cooperation, training, and exercises with the Baltic states within the framework of PFP, as well as provide practical assistance to the Baltic states of the kind that was extended to Poland, Hungary, and the Czech Republic after they received invitations to join NATO.

- The United States should work to the extent possible to defuse Russian security concerns by encouraging greater regional cooperation between Russia and the Baltic states. However, Russia should not be given a veto over the alliance's decision-making or over the right of the Baltic states to choose their own security orientation.

Russia

- Together with its European allies, the United States should press Russia to renounce officially the fiction that the Baltic states were incorporated "voluntarily" into the Soviet Union in 1940. Such a renunciation would greatly contribute to the normalization and development of Russian-Baltic relations over the long run.

- The United States should encourage Russia to sign the border agreements concluded with Estonia and Latvia.

- The social and economic problems of Kaliningrad, stemming from its physical separation from Russia, should be accorded a higher priority in U.S. policy. However, given Russian sensitivities, the United States should encourage others, especially the EU and the Nordics, to play the leading role. Poland and Lithuania should also be encouraged to continue to address Kaliningrad's mounting economic problems.

- To the extent possible, U.S. economic assistance should be channeled directly to the regions in northwestern Russia rather than going through Moscow. This would ensure that the assistance actually goes to local entities and NGOs rather than into the pockets of the central authorities.

- More U.S. assistance should be directed toward improving Russian-Baltic regional cooperation. At present, the bulk of U.S. assistance is directed toward nuclear-waste management in the Kola Peninsula rather than to promoting Russian-Baltic regional cooperation.

- The United States should use PFP to engage the Russians in the Baltic region. PFP provides an important vehicle for engaging the Russians and drawing them into closer regional cooperation. This can help to reduce Russia's sense of isolation and diminish its fears over the long term that this cooperation is directed against Russian security interests.

- The United States should encourage the Baltic states to continue to interact with Russia and not turn their backs on Moscow despite the economic crisis. Russia's integration into a regional framework can have important benefits for regional stability over the long run.

FINDINGS AND RECOMMENDATIONS

INTRODUCTION

The Independent Task Force on U.S. Policy Toward Northeastern Europe sponsored by the Council on Foreign Relations was formed to examine the policy challenges confronting the United States in northeastern Europe and recommend measures to advance U.S. interests in the region. The Task Force felt that northeastern Europe deserves special attention for several reasons.

First, during the Cold War, northeastern Europe was a strategic backwater and received relatively little attention in U.S. policy. However, since the end of the Cold War, the region has become an important focal point of U.S. policy. The Clinton administration has given northeastern Europe high priority and viewed the region as a laboratory for promoting closer regional cooperation and reknitting Europe—both East and West—into a more cohesive economic and political unit. As Secretary of State Madeleine Albright noted in her speech in Vilnius, Lithuania, in July 1997, "Our challenge is to build a fully integrated Europe that includes every European democracy willing to meet its responsibilities. That includes the Baltic nations." Thus, to some extent, northeastern Europe can be seen as a test case for the Clinton administration's general approach toward post–Cold War Europe.

Second, northeastern Europe is also a test case for the administration's policy toward Russia. One of the key elements of the administration's policy has been its efforts to reach out to Russia and to include Russia in regional cooperation schemes in northeastern Europe. This effort has been designed to integrate Russia gradually into a broader European framework as well as to defuse Russian concerns about the integration of the Baltic states into Euro-Atlantic institutions, especially NATO. It is seen by the administration as a litmus test of its effort to overcome the old zero-sum Cold War paradigm and demonstrate that greater regional cooperation can bring benefits to all, including Russia. Thus, how well this policy succeeds will have broader implications for the administration's policy toward Russia as a whole.

Third, three critical areas of U.S. policy interest—the Baltics, the Nordics, and Russia—intersect in northeastern Europe. Instability in the region would affect all three interests. Moreover, the Baltic region is the one region in Europe where a U.S.-Russian confrontation is still conceivable. Thus, the United States has a strong interest in defusing the potential for conflict in the region and promoting the region's stable economic and political development.

Fourth, the United States faces a number of critical challenges in the region. One of the most important is managing the security aspirations of the Baltic states. The Baltic states are tied to Europe historically and culturally. They share Western values and aspirations. Having thrown off the shackles of communism and Russian domination, the Baltic states, like their counterparts in Central Europe, want to join Europe and Euro-Atlantic institutions. How the United States seeks to accommodate their security aspirations will be a major test of the U.S. commitment to creating a "Europe whole and free" and its ability to overcome the zero-sum logic of the Cold War.

Fifth, the policy challenges in northeastern Europe—particularly those in the Baltic subregion—directly touch on Russia's security concerns and have important implications for U.S.-Russian relations. Top Russian officials have reiterated that Baltic membership in NATO could have serious repercussions for Russia's relations with NATO and the newly established Russia-NATO Council in particular. Such statements should not necessarily be taken at face value. But they highlight the sensitivity of the Baltic issue among the Russian policy elite and ensure that it will remain a highly contentious issue in U.S.-Russian relations.

The issue of Kaliningrad complicates the policy challenges in northeastern Europe. With the independence of the Baltic states, Kaliningrad has become an enclave cut off from the main Russian territory. As Poland and the Baltic states become more integrated into Euro-Atlantic institutions, Kaliningrad's situation will become more and more of an anomaly. Ties to the Baltic states and Europe are likely to increase, especially in the economic area, and pressures by the local elites in Kaliningrad for greater autonomy and closer association with Europe are likely to grow, accentuating Moscow's security concerns. In addition, Kaliningrad has become a major center of crime, drug trafficking, and arms smuggling. As a result, Kaliningrad could become an increasing source of regional tension and concern over the next decade.

Sixth, the issue of security in northeastern Europe directly affects U.S. relations with the Nordic states, especially Sweden and Finland. The Baltic states are in the Nordic states' strategic backyard. Thus, how the Baltic issue is handled has direct implications for their security—and especially for the relations of the Nordic states with Russia. Neither Sweden nor Finland wants to see the Baltic or Nordic region become some kind of a gray zone or flash point. At the same time, neither wants to assume the primary responsibility for the security of the Baltic states, which would overburden the capability of either country.

Finally, security issues in northeastern Europe pose important dilemmas for U.S. policy toward NATO. The Baltic issue is the trickiest and most sensitive part of the enlargement puzzle. The Clinton administration has committed itself to helping the Baltic states gain membership in NATO. But many U.S. senators have reservations about the wisdom of further enlargement, especially to the Baltic states. Many U.S. allies also have reservations about Baltic membership in NATO—in particular because of fears about its impact on relations with Russia as well as broader concerns about the implications for NATO military coherence and effectiveness. Thus, gaining support for Baltic membership could be difficult and put additional strains on U.S. relations with its allies in NATO.

In short, far from being a strategic backwater, northeastern Europe is emerging as an important area of strategic interest and concern for the United States. Developments there could directly affect U.S. relations with the Nordics, the Baltic states, the European Union, NATO, and Russia. Moreover, several elements of the Clinton administration's policy toward the region—especially its support for Baltic membership in NATO—are highly controversial. The administration's policy, however, has not been subject to much debate or public scrutiny. With this in mind, the members of the Task Force felt that a systematic examination of U.S. policy toward northeastern Europe was both important and timely and could contribute to a better understanding of the challenges that the United States faces in this strategically important region.

U.S. POLICY TOWARD NORTHEASTERN EUROPE

Prior to 1990, it was difficult to speak of a U.S. policy toward northeastern Europe. U.S. policy tended to be conducted along Cold War lines, with different policies being pursued toward Denmark and Norway, which were members of NATO; Sweden and Finland, which were neutral; and the Baltic states, which were part of the former Soviet Union. However, since the end of the Cold War—and particularly since the arrival of the Clinton administration—the contours of a regional policy toward northeastern Europe gradually have begun to emerge.

The Clinton administration has given northeastern Europe high priority and has sought to develop a coherent overall policy toward the region. That policy has been designed to enhance stability and security in northeastern Europe and help overcome the Cold War divisions by promoting greater regional cooperation. This effort to promote a truly regional policy has been one of the distinctive features of the Clinton administration's approach to northeastern Europe.

The cornerstone of the administration's policy is the Northern European Initiative (NEI). The initiative, launched in Bergen (Norway) in September 1997, is designed to capitalize on recent changes and opportunities in northeastern Europe that have arisen as a result of the end of the Cold War. It seeks to promote an economically and socially unified region—including northwestern Russia—and foster stronger regional cooperation and cross-border ties, relying not only on governments but also on the private sector and nongovernmental organizations (NGOs).

The administration's policy toward northeastern Europe has proceeded along three separate but closely related tracks. The first track has been designed to integrate the Baltic states into Euro-Atlantic institutions and structures, including NATO. This track has been regarded by the administration as a critical test of its ability to overcome the old zero-sum logic of the Cold War and as a key element of its effort to enhance stability in Europe as a whole. It is also the most controversial and sensitive element of the administration's policy because of its potential impact on relations with Russia.

The administration's Baltic policy has evolved gradually and incrementally. An important step in its development was the decision to create a new office of Nordic and Baltic Affairs within the Bureau of European and Canadian Affairs in the State Department. This was a very important symbolic move; it underscored that policy toward the Baltic states was considered to be an integral part of U.S. policy toward Europe, not toward the former Soviet Union.

Soon thereafter, the State Department developed the Baltic Action Plan. The plan was designed to strengthen bilateral ties with the Baltic states and promote closer cooperation in a number of political, economic, and security areas. At the same time, the plan carefully avoided addressing the most controversial and tension-provoking issue: NATO membership.

The administration took another important step with the enunciation of the Charter of Partnership, or "Baltic Charter," which was signed with the Baltic states in January 1998. The Charter builds on the Baltic Action Plan but goes much further in addressing the Baltic states' security concerns. It makes clear that the Baltic states will not be excluded from Euro-Atlantic organizations and structures simply because of geography (i.e., their proximity to Russia) or the fact that they were once part of the former Soviet Union. Although the Charter does not contain a security guarantee, the United States committed itself in the Charter to help create the conditions for eventual Baltic membership in NATO.

This pledge is a touchstone of the administration's policy. But it is not the only element. The administration has also pledged to take steps to promote closer economic ties with the Baltic states and facilitate their entry into the World Trade Organization and European Union. Bilateral working groups have been set up in energy, telecommunications, transportation, and the environment. The first Partnership meeting in Riga in July 1998 also included a private-sector initiative to improve the business and investment climate in the three states.

In addition, the administration has undertaken a major study of the defense needs of each of the Baltic states (the "Kievenaar Study"). The study identifies current weaknesses and sets priorities to help these countries modernize their military forces so that they will be more compatible with those of NATO. The Baltic states are currently incorporating many of the guidelines in the study into their defense planning. The administration has also taken the lead, along with Denmark, in coordinating military assistance to these countries through the Baltic Security Assistance Group (BALTSEA). These initiatives are designed to help the Baltic states become strong candidates for NATO membership by ensuring that they will be "producers" of security, not simply "consumers" of it.

Finally, the United States has encouraged efforts at social integration in support of the Organization for Security and Cooperation in Europe's (OSCE) recommendations on citizenship. These efforts have been designed to promote inclusiveness and reconciliation and to help integrate the Russian minority more fully into Baltic political and social life. The social integration of the Russian minority is an important prerequisite for long-term political stability in the Baltic states as well as for those nations' good relations with Russia. Under prodding from the United States and its European allies, Latvia and Estonia have recently taken steps to bring their citizenship laws into conformity with European norms—an important prerequisite for EU and NATO membership. In addition, the administration has encouraged the Baltic states to make an honest reckoning with their past, including the Holocaust. All three Baltic states, for instance, have recently set up national historical commissions to deal with crimes committed under Nazi and totalitarian rule.

The second track of the administration's policy is designed to strengthen relations with the Nordic states and coordinate efforts to improve regional cooperation. It focuses on six major areas: law enforcement, the environment, energy, public health, strengthening civil courts, and business promotion. The administration has also worked closely with the Nordic countries, Britain, and Germany to promote military assistance to the Baltic states through BALTSEA.

These initiatives have given relations with the Nordic countries an unusual intensity and warmth. Indeed, relations with the Nordic states are better today than they have been at any time since the end of World War II. In particular, relations with Finland and Sweden, two former neutrals, have been strengthened. The United States has worked closely with both countries, for instance, to produce a prototype interim fuel-storage cask in the Kola Peninsula as well as cooperated with them in the Great Lakes/Baltic Sea Partnership for environmental cleanup.

The United States and Sweden are also cooperating on two civilian-military environmental programs in Latvia and Lithuania: a base management plan at a former Soviet tank and artillery site in Adazi, Latvia; and the development of a regional defense and environmental training center at the Nemencine Civil Defense Training Center in Lithuania. In addition, Sweden has indicated it will play a major role in the implementation of a program of work on water management under the Great Lakes/Baltic Sea Partnership.

This cooperation with the Nordic countries, particularly Finland and Sweden, has given the administration's policy a broader regional focus. It has also helped to make the policy more palatable to Russia. Finally, it has served to link the issue of Baltic and Nordic security more closely to the broader issue of European security and ensure that the two issues are not decoupled (a strong Nordic and Baltic concern).

The third track has been marked by an effort to encourage Russia's greater participation and involvement in regional cooperation. Promoting Russia's integration in regional cooperation is predicated on the belief that the more Russia is integrated into northeastern Europe, the more likely it is to integrate smoothly into the rest of Europe. The third track is also designed to help defuse Russian anxieties about the membership of the Baltic states in Euro-Atlantic institutions. In the administration's view, the Baltics should become a gateway for cooperation and Russia's broader integration into European institutions.

Particular attention has been focused on developing cooperation with northwestern Russia—again within a broader regional framework and working closely with the Nordic countries. The main vehicle for promoting this policy has been the NEI, which is designed to promote cross-border initiatives in areas such as trade and investment, institution building, energy management, infrastructure enhancement, nuclear-waste control, law enforcement, and the development of civil society.

Taken together, these three tracks represent an ambitious agenda. The administration, however, faces a number of important obstacles in implementing this agenda.

First, it is not clear whether the administration's policy is domestically sustainable. Some aspects of the policy—especially Baltic membership in NATO—are highly controversial. Many U.S. senators are skeptical about the merits of further enlargement, especially to the Baltic states. The administration therefore will need to build a domestic constituency for its policy—something it has yet to do.

Second, many of America's European allies have reservations about Baltic membership in NATO—largely because of concerns about the impact on Russia. A number of the allies, especially France and Italy, have already signaled that they believe that the next round of enlargement should be oriented toward the south and be designed to stabilize southeastern Europe. Thus, the administration (or its successor) will have to build a coalition within the alliance in support of its policy.

Third, Russia strongly opposes Baltic membership in NATO. Thus, unless skillfully managed, the administration's policy could lead to a serious deterioration of relations with Russia.

Finally, there is the question of resources. The administration has staked out an ambitious agenda. But it has committed relatively few resources to carry out this agenda. Without a more robust commitment of resources, many of the projects under the NEI may languish or not be implemented. In addition, the United States will have a hard time persuading other countries and organizations, especially the Nordics and the EU, to allocate more resources for joint projects.

IS NORTHEASTERN EUROPE A REGION?

Another critical question related to the administration's policy is whether northeastern Europe really is a coherent region. On historical grounds, there are strong reasons to see northeastern Europe as a region. Historically, the countries around the Baltic Sea have had close links, especially in the economic area. In the thirteenth and sixteenth centuries, the Hanseatic League played an important role in knitting the region together both economically and politically.

The Cold War created an artificial division of Europe—including northeastern Europe—which weakened traditional trade patterns and political links, especially with the Baltic states. With the end of the Cold War, however, traditional regional and subregional ties have begun to reemerge. The Baltic states have begun to reorient their trade toward Europe, especially with the Nordic countries. At the same time, traditional political associations have been strengthened. Estonia, for instance, has established a special relationship with Finland, while Lithuania has strengthened ties to Poland.

Regional cooperation has also been strengthened. Northeastern Europe today has some of the best-functioning regional and subregional institutions. The Council of Baltic Sea States (CBSS), the Barents Euro-Arctic Council (BEAC), and the Nordic Council have helped to knit northeastern Europe more closely together and enhance greater regional cooperation and stability. The CBSS and the BEAC also include Russia, thereby drawing Russia more closely into regional structures.

Perhaps the most controversial aspect of the administration's approach to northeastern Europe relates to Russia's role. Is Russia a part of the region—or simply an object of regional policy? This issue is all the more important because, as noted, one of the main goals of the Clinton administration's Northern European Initiative has been to promote closer regional cooperation with Russia and draw Russia more deeply into regional structures in the area.

Historically, regions in northwestern Russia such as St. Petersburg, Murmansk, and Novgorod maintained close links with the Nordic and Baltic states and were part of a northeast European economic sphere. In this sense, one can say that these parts of Russia do have close historical ties with the Nordic and Baltic region. At the same time, however, Russia's political, social, and economic evolution has differed in significant ways from that of the Baltic and Nordic states. Democratic institutions and elements of a market economy have weaker roots in Russia. This makes Russia's involvement and integration into northeastern Europe problematic.

Psychologically and politically, Russia has yet to decide what type of a relationship it wants with the region—one of dominance or one of mutual respect and equality. Many Russians continue to see the Baltic states as a part of Russia's sphere of influence. Russian officials have sought to draw a "red line" in the Baltics regarding NATO enlargement and have often used the issue of the Russian minority in the Baltic states as a means of exerting pressure on the Baltic nations when it has proved politically convenient to do so.

Economically, moreover, it is hard to integrate Russia into regional cooperation schemes because of the slow pace of reform in Russia and the lack of a strong legal framework that would encourage and protect Western investment. The Clinton administration's Northern European Initiative seeks to promote greater regional economic cooperation. But although many of the Russian regional elites want Western investment, they have done little to create a legal framework that would attract it. Until they do, it will be difficult to attract large-scale Western investment.

In addition, much of the capital that is available for development is not subject to strict fiscal control. Hence, many Baltic states are wary of cooperating too closely with Russia, for fear this will increase the involvement of Russian criminal groups within their territories. Finally, the Russian financial crisis has further diminished the prospects for regional economic cooperation. Trade between Russia and the Baltic states has declined since August 1998, and any growth in trade is likely to be limited in the near future. Industries such as food processing and fisheries have been particularly hard hit.

This suggests that any effort to integrate Russia into the region and to promote regional cooperation with Russia will be difficult. Despite these difficulties, however, the effort to involve Russia more closely in regional cooperation in northeastern Europe should not be abandoned. The more Russia is integrated into the region, the greater its stake in regional stability is likely to be and the easier it will be to defuse Russian anxieties about the Baltic states' desires for close ties to NATO in the long run.

Russia needs to see the Baltic region not as a pathway to aggression but rather as an opportunity—that is, a gateway to greater cooperation and European integration. The goal of U.S. policy should be to help Russia make this psychological adjustment. Involving Russia—especially northwestern Russia—in closer regional cooperation schemes can facilitate and accelerate that process.

Such a policy, moreover, is in keeping with long-term trends in Russia. As central power weakens, the regions are likely to become increasingly more important. Indeed, some regions have already begun to develop their own foreign and economic policies. This trend seems likely to be strengthened in the future, as more and more power devolves, by default, to the regions.

The problem is that the diffusion of power so far has not created strong regions. It has led instead to both a weak center *and* weak regions. The central authorities have proven increasingly incapable of providing for the needs of the regions, but, at the same time, the regions are too weak to provide for their own needs. The recent food crisis in Kaliningrad, a region almost totally dependent on outside exports and assistance to meet its food needs, underscores this problem.

The local elites, especially in northwestern Russia, want greater regional cooperation and Western investment. This can help them to meet their local needs, currently neglected by the center.

The central authorities, however, remain highly suspicious of Western ties to the regions, which they fear will weaken their power and possibly spark separatist tendencies. (This is particularly true in the case of Kaliningrad.)

This poses a difficult dilemma for U.S. policy. Over the long term, a greater devolution of power to the regions seems likely, even inevitable. This argues for increasing ties and assistance to the regions. At the same time, the United States needs to be careful to avoid giving the impression that it is encouraging separatist tendencies. This could exacerbate suspicions in Moscow that the United States is consciously trying to promote the disintegration of Russia.

Moreover, the United States has a strong interest in ensuring that the center maintains control over certain functions, especially the control of nuclear weapons and military forces. It would not be in the U.S. interest to see the emergence of regional satraps with their own military forces and nuclear arsenals. Hence, in pursuing its policy the United States will need to tread a fine line between encouraging regional ties and cooperation and helping the Russian state to maintain control over essential military and security functions.

BALTIC SECURITY

The Baltic issue is one of the most difficult and sensitive parts of the security equation in northeastern Europe. The key policy dilemma is how to provide for the security of the Baltic states without provoking a crisis with Russia or weakening Western institutions. The Clinton administration is committed to helping the Baltic states join Euro-Atlantic institutions, including NATO. It sees this as an integral part of its "open door" policy and its effort to promote integration in Europe.

The administration's support for Baltic membership in NATO, however, is highly controversial and has not been subjected to much systematic scrutiny or debate. As noted earlier, many U.S. senators have reservations about a new round of enlargement in the near future, especially one that would include the Baltic states. Thus, getting congressional support for such a policy will not be easy. Moreover, many European allies also have reservations about Baltic membership.

Clearly, the issue of Baltic membership in NATO needs to be carefully managed in order to ensure that it contributes to the broader goals of enhancing regional and European security. At the same time, the rationale behind enlargement needs to be clearly understood. Enlargement is not being carried out because there is a military threat but rather as part of a broader process of extending stability to the East and expanding the European geopolitical space. The Baltic region should not be excluded from this process simply because it lies close to Russia.

The opponents of Baltic membership in NATO make several arguments. The first is Russian opposition. Russia has tried to draw a "red line" against enlargement to the Baltic states and warned that Baltic membership would cause a crisis in Russia's relationship with NATO and jeopardize cooperation within the newly established Russia-NATO Council (Permanent Joint Council). Why risk that? opponents argue. The costs of Baltic membership outweigh the benefits.

Clearly, the administration has to take Russian concerns seriously. But this is quite different from taking Russian objections at face value or accepting their validity. That would be tantamount to accepting that the Baltic states are in the Russian sphere of influence and that Russia has a de facto veto over the security orientation of the Baltic states—and over NATO decision-making. No country should be excluded from joining an alliance or an international organization simply because it was once part of the former Soviet Union.

Moreover, a strong argument can be made that Baltic membership in NATO would help cure Russia of its imperial nostalgia. As long as the Baltic states are not included in NATO, Russia is likely to view them as part of its sphere of influence and attempt to constrain their security options. The best way to stabilize the Baltic region and get Russia to accept the Baltic countries as fully sovereign and independent states is to take the Baltic issue off the table and include the Baltic states in NATO.

This does not mean that the Baltic states should be immediately admitted into NATO. Russia will need time to adjust to the new strategic realities and absorb the impact of the first round of enlargement. It would be unwise and dangerous to back Russia into a corner or to overburden the Russian agenda, particularly at this delicate moment. But the basic principles of the "open door" and no "red lines" should be strongly reaffirmed. The actual timing of Baltic entry will depend on many factors—not the least of which will be the performance of the Baltic states in meeting the requirements for membership, including in the military field.

A second objection to Baltic membership often raised by opponents is that the Baltic states are "indefensible," and thus NATO should not extend an Article V commitment to them that it cannot carry out. Clearly, on their own, the Baltic states could not prevent an invasion by a major power like Russia. But with proper training and acting in concert, they could raise the cost of an invasion to any potential aggressor and buy time for outside reinforcements.

Moreover, there is an important difference between defensibility and protectability. During the Cold War, Copenhagen and Berlin were not defensible in a strict military sense. But the Alliance maintained a commitment to defend them. The Soviet Union was deterred from any overt military aggression by the knowledge that any military action against Copenhagen or Berlin would prompt a large-scale military response by the West. Thus, whether NATO could defend the Baltic states in a strict military sense may be less important than making clear that any effort by Russia to use force in the Baltics would prompt a strong response by NATO against highly valued Russian assets. This could serve to deter Russia from taking military action against the Baltic states.

Furthermore, enlargement of NATO to the Baltic states need not involve the stationing of Western combat troops or nuclear weapons on Baltic soil. NATO did not station combat troops or nuclear weapons in Norway—which shares a border with Russia—during the Cold War and has consciously refrained from doing so in Poland, Hungary, and the Czech Republic as well. It could pursue the same policy in the Baltic states. As in the case of the three newly admitted members, it could make clear in advance that it has no intention of stationing combat troops or nuclear weapons on Baltic soil as long as the security environment remains benign. This could help to defuse Russian security concerns.

A third argument often cited by opponents is the presence of a large Russian minority on the territory of the Baltic states and unresolved minority issues between Russia and several of those states, especially Latvia and Estonia. This argument, however, is much weaker today than it was a few years ago. Both Latvia and Estonia have recently relaxed their citizenship laws and brought them in conformity with European norms. This has helped to dampen tensions with Russia and made it much harder for Russia to claim credibly that there is widespread discrimination against the Russian minority.

The real problem today is not the lack of laws protecting the rights of the Russian minority but the implementation of the laws already on the books. Implementation has been hindered, in particular, by lack of money, especially for the training of language teachers in the Russian-speaking areas. This is an area to which the United States should devote greater attention—and more resources.

Finally, opponents point to the low military capability of the Baltic states. Defense spending in the Baltic states, especially Latvia, is well below that of most NATO members. Equipment and training are also below NATO standards—primarily because, unlike the other states in Central and Eastern Europe, the Baltic states have had to build their armies from scratch.

However, the Baltic states have recently begun to address these deficiencies. Lithuania passed a law in January 1999 that commits it to raise defense spending to 1.95–2.00 percent of gross domestic product by 2001. Estonia has also agreed to increase its defense spending to 2 percent by the year 2002. The real problem is Latvia, where defense spending is below 1 percent.

In addition, the three Baltic states have taken a number of steps to strengthen defense cooperation and enhance their ability to operate effectively with NATO forces. The most important and successful initiative has been the creation of a joint Baltic Peacekeeping Battalion (BALTBAT). Composed of battalions from all three Baltic states, BALTBAT has been deployed in Bosnia as part of the Nordic Brigade. The joint peacekeeping battalion is an important expression of the Baltic states' readiness to contribute to international peacekeeping. At the same time, it has helped the Baltic states gain valuable experience in working closely with NATO.

Several other joint efforts at defense cooperation have also been initiated. A joint naval squadron (BALTRON), to be based in Estonia, has been set up; a joint Baltic airspace surveillance system (BALTNET), to be based in Lithuania, is also being established. And a joint Baltic Defense College (BALTDEFCOL), has been set up in Tartu, Estonia.

Given the economic constraints the Baltic countries face, they cannot afford a massive military buildup. But such a buildup is not strategically necessary since the security environment at the moment remains relatively benign. Hence, the Baltics have time to develop their military forces. They should be encouraged to pursue a balanced approach. The main emphasis in the initial phase should be on personnel and training, not weapons procurement.

To avoid the complications associated with NATO membership, some observers have suggested that the Nordic countries should assume responsibility for the security of the Baltic states. The Nordic countries, however, reject this approach. They do not want to see Baltic security decoupled from European security. This is also the reason they have rejected Russian calls for creating a special security zone in the Baltics. Moreover, a Nordic security guarantee, as the Nordic and Baltic states well know, would not be credible.

Others have suggested that the Baltic states should join the EU—but not NATO—and that this would solve their security problems. Clearly, membership in the EU would help diminish the prospect of outside attack or intimidation. Once they were members of the EU, any attempt by Russia to put pressure on the Baltic states would have serious implications for Russia's relations with the EU.

However, in the event of a serious threat to the security of any Baltic state, the EU does not have the military capability—at least not at the moment—to respond. It would have to turn to NATO. Thus, in the case of a serious threat to the Baltic states NATO would eventually become involved.

In short, Baltic membership in NATO can contribute to regional and European security. *But it needs to be managed prudently and be part of a broader strategy to enhance stability in northeastern Europe.* In pursuit of such a strategy, the administration should:

- *Use the Partnership for Peace (PFP) to increase interoperability and help prepare the Baltic states for NATO membership.* PFP provides an important mechanism for enhancing the ability of the Baltic states to operate more effectively with NATO and for helping them prepare for NATO membership. The United States should increase the number of PFP exercises with the Baltic states as well as provide practical assistance of the kind extended to the three newest members (Poland, Hungary, and the Czech Republic) after they received invitations.

- *Encourage the EU to put Latvia and Lithuania on the fast track to EU membership along with Estonia.* This could provide important reassurance to the Baltic states and act as an important deterrent to Russian pressure or intimidation. It would also relieve some of the pressure for membership in NATO in the short term. This, in turn, would help reduce Russian anxieties and allow the NATO issue to be managed in a less intense atmosphere.

- *Defuse Russian security concerns through enhanced regional cooperation, including in the military field.* The more Russia is integrated into broader regional cooperation, the less nervous it is likely to be about Baltic membership in NATO over the long run. This is particularly true in the military field. PFP provides an important vehicle for engaging the Russians and drawing them more closely into regional cooperation.

- *Build a domestic constituency for Baltic membership in NATO.* The administration needs to make the case for Baltic membership more strongly with Congress and particularly to clarify the issue of the timing of any Baltic entry into NATO. Otherwise gaining congressional support for admitting the Baltic states may prove difficult.

- *Forge a consensus within the alliance for Baltic membership in NATO.* The administration will need to create a coalition within the alliance for Baltic membership. Denmark, Norway, Poland, and Iceland can be counted as strong supporters. But they are not enough. The administration will have to gain the support of key allies, especially Germany, Britain, and France.

- *Encourage the Baltic states to integrate the Russian minority more completely into Baltic political and social life.* The more the Russian minority is integrated into Baltic society, the less of an internal problem it is likely to be and the less Russia will be able to exploit the minority issue for foreign policy purposes.

- *Encourage the Baltic states to address their past more forthrightly.* NATO is not just a military organization. It is also about values. As part of their effort to demonstrate their commitment to Western values, the Baltic countries need an honest reckoning with their past, including the Holocaust. They have taken the first step in this regard with the establishment of national historical commissions to deal with crimes committed under Nazi and totalitarian rule. However, these commissions need to be more than just formalities. They must address the crimes in a forthright and honest way. This would help to build bridges to various parts of the American political spectrum and clearly demonstrate that the Baltic countries are committed to Western values.

SHOULD THE BALTIC STATES BE TREATED AS A GROUP?

One of the key policy issues facing the United States in approaching the question of Baltic membership in Euro-Atlantic institutions is whether to treat the Baltic states as a group or to devise separate policies for each of them. The three Baltic states are often seen as a package, largely because they were forcibly incorporated into the Soviet Union at the same time and are geographically close to one another. However, although the three states share some things in common, they are actually quite different.

Estonia is the most advanced economically. Early in the reform process, Estonia adopted a currency board that eliminates most of the discretionary power of monetary authorities to stimulate the economy. It also established a highly liberal foreign trade regime and refused to pay full refunds to depositors in failed banks. Estonia has also introduced an extensive privatization program and has been able to attract the most foreign investment.

Estonia has greatly benefited from its proximity to Finland, which has acted as its patron. However, the existence of a large Russian minority—nearly 30 percent of Estonia's population—has complicated relations with Russia, which continues to claim that the Russian population faces systematic discrimination by Estonia as a result of stringent citizenship laws introduced in 1991 and 1992. These laws, however, have been amended subsequently to conform to OSCE and EU norms.

Latvia's situation is somewhat different. With its three ports, it is a major center for Russian trade, especially oil exports. It is also the most Russified of the three Baltic republics and the worst hit by corruption and Mafia activities. The Russian community accounts for nearly 40 percent of Latvia's population and almost half of the population of Riga, where it dominates the business activities, especially trade with Russia. The degree of Russian influence in the economy is worrysome to many Latvians, who fear that Russia may indirectly seek to subvert Latvia by controlling its economy.

Lithuania is more of a Central European country than the other two Baltic states and was for centuries dominated by Poland. For historical-cultural reasons, it has tended to look increasingly to Poland for support in its efforts to establish closer ties to Euro-Atlantic institutions, especially NATO. The two countries signed a treaty of friendship and cooperation in 1993, and recently they have set up a joint peacekeeping battalion.

Lithuania is also a much more homogeneous society—80 percent of the population is Lithuanian. The Russian minority is relatively small (less than 9 percent of the population). This has made it easier for Lithuania than for Estonia and Latvia to regulate its relations with Russia. It has also given Lithuanian politics a high degree of coherence and stability. Because of the high levels of homogeneity of the population, Lithuanian politicians have been free to concentrate on issues and ideologies instead of being preoccupied with ethnic issues, as in Estonia and Latvia.

In the last few years, the Baltic region's initial solidarity of the early post-1991 period has begun to erode. Estonia has increasingly sought to pursue a separate path in relations with the EU, while Lithuania has tried to hitch its wagon more closely to Poland's star in the hope that this would improve its chances to gain entry into NATO. Latvia, on the other hand, has lacked a clear Western patron (though Sweden has tended to play this role by default). This has left Riga feeling somewhat isolated.

The EU's decision to open accession negotiations with Estonia in early 1998 has accelerated the process of differentiation. Over the long run, Estonia seems likely to look increasingly to the Nordic states, especially Finland, while Lithuania will probably seek closer ties to Central Europe, especially Poland. If this trend continues, it could increase Latvia's isolation, since, as noted, Latvia lacks a clear Western patron and is more dependent on Russia economically than Estonia or Lithuania.

This increasing process of differentiation strengthens the case for the United States to differentiate between the three Baltic states in its own policy, particularly regarding NATO enlargement. It might be useful, therefore, to consider including one Baltic state in a second round of enlargement, provided it meets the responsibilities for membership. This would underscore to Moscow that there are no "red lines" and anchor the Baltic states more firmly into Euro-Atlantic institutions. At the same time, Moscow would find it easier to accept one new member than membership for all three Baltic states at once.

Which of the three Baltic states should be included in the next round of NATO enlargement will depend, to a large extent, on which one is best able to meet the responsibilities of membership at the time. At present, Lithuania has made the most progress in modernizing its military forces. It also has the best relations with Moscow. Thus, its inclusion would provide the least controversy with Russia.

The risk of such a policy is that it would leave the other two Baltic states more exposed and might give Russia the impression that they have been relegated to the Russian sphere of influence. This would be less of a problem for Estonia, since it is on the fast track for EU membership, than for Latvia. Latvia poses a special problem for several reasons. It has the largest Russian minority. Its economy is also more tightly interwoven with the Russian economy. And it lacks a clear Western patron. Moreover, its internal weaknesses reduce the prospects that it will become a member of the EU or NATO in the near future.

Thus, if Lithuania were to be included in a second round of NATO enlargement and Estonia is included in the first round of EU enlargement, some special measures ought to be taken to reduce Latvia's exposure and bind it more closely into a Euro-Atlantic framework. One possibility would be to encourage the EU to put Latvia on the fast track to EU membership, along with Estonia, since its economic performance is nearly as good as Estonia's. In addition, the United States, the Nordics, and the EU should step up support and assistance for reform in Latvia. This would help to anchor Latvia more tightly to the West and reduce its vulnerability to outside pressure.

THE NORDIC CONNECTION

The Nordic countries—Denmark, Norway, Sweden, and Finland—represent important potential partners for the United States in its effort to develop a coherent regional strategy toward northeastern Europe. All are globally oriented, outward-looking countries. They also have a strong stake in strengthening stability and security in northeastern Europe, especially the Baltic region.

The Nordic states, however, are not a homogeneous group. Within NATO, Denmark has been the most ardent champion of the Baltic cause. It has played a leading role in providing the Baltic states with financial and low-level military assistance. It has also been the driving force behind the establishment of BALTBAT. Baltic platoons have been integrated into the Danish peacekeeping battalion in Croatia and are also included in the Nordic brigade in IFOR/SFOR.

Norway has shown less interest in the Baltic issue. It regards itself primarily as an Atlantic, not a Baltic country. Moreover, it has an important security agenda with Russia, and it has not wanted the Baltic issue to interfere with that bilateral agenda. However, recently Norway has begun to take a more active interest in Baltic security issues.

Finland and Sweden have both provided considerable military assistance to the Baltic states. But here, too, there have been notable differences. Finland has tended to favor Estonia in its assistance to the Baltic states. Sweden's policy, on the other hand, has been more evenhanded, and unlike Finland, it has tried to avoid singling out any one Baltic country for special treatment.

Some Western analysts and officials have suggested that the Nordic countries ought to assume primary responsibility for the security of the Baltic countries. The Nordic countries, however, reject such an approach. They do not want to see Nordic and Baltic security decoupled from European security. Moreover, a Nordic security guarantee would not be very credible—a fact that they and the Baltic states clearly understand.

Sweden and Finland also want strong U.S. involvement in the Baltic region. This is not only because of their desire to avoid overexposure but also because of the economic, political, and military assets that the United States brings to the table. U.S. involvement creates an environment that makes it easier for Sweden and Finland to be more deeply engaged with the Baltic states. Thus, while the United States needs to consult with Sweden and Finland in developing its Baltic policy, it cannot count on them to assume the main responsibility for Baltic security.

At the same time, the end of the Cold War has eroded the concept of neutrality and raised new security dilemmas for Sweden and Finland. Both countries have taken important steps away from neutrality by joining the EU and PFP. Although neither country has officially expressed a desire to join NATO, in both countries a debate has emerged behind the scenes among policy elites and journalists about the possibility of eventual NATO membership.

This debate has gone furthest in Finland. Some Finnish commentators have suggested that Finland will have little choice but to join NATO, not because Finland faces any particular threat to its sovereignty but in order to ensure that it has a "seat at the table" on matters that directly affect Finnish security interests. The Finnish government, however, has continued to argue that it sees no reason for now to change Finland's policy of military nonalignment. At the same time, it has been careful not to exclude the option of NATO membership at a later date.

The debate in Sweden has been more muted. However, voices in the media and the Moderate Party have begun to raise the issue of NATO membership. Carl Bildt, the leader of the Moderate Party, has openly called for Sweden to join NATO. The need for defense cuts has also caused some members of the Swedish policy elite to question whether Sweden can afford to remain outside the alliance over the long run.

The development of a European Security and Defense Identity (ESDI) and NATO's growing involvement in operations beyond its current borders could serve to erode the Swedish and Finnish commitments to military nonalignment even further. To date, Sweden and Finland have not been pressed too hard to change their security policies because ESDI has been only a gleam in the eye of EU policymakers. But if Britain and France really act on their December 4, 1998, declaration in Saint-Malo to develop a more robust ESDI, both Sweden and Finland could come under stronger pressure from their European allies in the EU to revise their defense policies and abandon their military nonalignment. Once they joined ESDI, there would be less reason not to join NATO.

This is not to suggest that Finland or Sweden are about to join NATO in the near future. But the security outlook in both countries is shifting, as each seeks to adjust to the changes unleashed by the end of the Cold War. Thus, the prospect of NATO membership for both countries over the long run can no longer be excluded entirely, particularly if Austria decides to apply for NATO membership, as it well could in a few years.

Finnish and Swedish membership in NATO would cast the whole Baltic issue in a new light. In particular, it could help to defuse the "defensibility" argument. If NATO were ready to assume an Article V commitment to Finland with its long border with Russia, then there would be less reason not to extend a similar guarantee to the Baltic states.

In the short term, however, there are strong advantages to having Sweden and Finland outside the alliance. Their non-membership provides a certain "cover" for the Baltic states and reduces their exposure and vulnerability. If Sweden and Finland were to join the alliance, many of the other objections to Baltic membership—Russia, the low level of Baltic military forces, diminished Alliance cohesion, and so on—would still exist. Moreover, with an early entry of Sweden and Finland into NATO, the Baltic states would be left more isolated and exposed. This could accentuate their security concerns.

Sweden and Finland will need time to sort out their security orientations and priorities. In the meantime, the United States may be better off trying to narrow the distinction between NATO members and nonmembers and intensifying military cooperation with the Baltic states in a variety of areas, particularly through enhanced PFP. This could help defuse the saliency of the membership issue and would buy time for the European security environment—and Russian attitudes—to evolve. Such an evolution, in turn, could make it easier to deal with the issue of Baltic membership later on.

Moreover, it may be useful to encourage the Nordics to take the lead—through BALTSEA—in providing military assistance to the Baltic states, with the United States playing a supporting backup role. This may appear less threatening to Moscow than if the United States plays a highly visible role. At the same time, it would ensure that the Baltic states receive the assistance they need to modernize their militaries.

THE RUSSIAN FACTOR

U.S. interests and policy in northeastern Europe will be significantly influenced by Russian behavior and policy in the region, especially toward the Baltic states. As former Swedish Prime Minister Carl Bildt has noted, Russia's willingness to accept the independence of the Baltic states is the real "litmus test" of the degree to which Russia has jettisoned its imperial ambitions.

Russia has always viewed the Baltic states differently from the other parts of the former Soviet Union. At the same time, it has tended to see the Baltic region as "special," both because of its geographic proximity to Russia and because the Baltic states were once part of the Soviet Union. Although Moscow has posed no objection to Baltic membership in the EU, it strongly opposes the incorporation of the Baltic states into NATO.

Relations between Russia and the Baltic states have been · strained by the treatment of the Russian minority, especially in Estonia and Latvia. This has been less of a problem in Lithuania, which has a much smaller Russian-speaking population (less than 9 percent). Unlike Estonia and Latvia, Lithuania granted automatic citizenship to the Russian minority. Estonia and Latvia, in contrast, have imposed special language and other requirements for citizenship on Russians who were not living in those countries prior to 1940. This has led Russian officials to levy charges of discrimination.

However, the minority issue has become less of a source of friction lately as a result of changes in the Estonian and Latvian citizenship laws that have brought them into accord with the norms of the EU and the OSCE. This has made it much harder for Russia to argue that the Russian minority in these countries is suffering from "massive discrimination" and "genocide," as it had previously claimed.

At the same time, it is important to recognize that Russian complaints about the Latvian and Estonian treatment of the Russian minority often are motivated by factors that have little to do with the situation of the minority. Many Russians, especially the nationalists, see the minority issue as a convenient means of pressuring the Baltic states and achieving broader political objectives. They are thus unlikely to drop the claims regardless of how much the situation of the minority improves.

Private economic interests also play an important role. The deterioration of Russian-Latvian relations in the spring of 1998, for instance, coincided with difficulties which the Russian oil consortium LUKoil was having in acquiring shares in Latvian harbor installations and with the decline in world oil prices. The sanctions imposed on Latvia by Russia in early 1998 had several objectives. They allowed the Russian government to curry favor with the nationalists. In addition, they represented a gesture to the oil industry, which, because of falling oil prices, had an interest in seeing a reduction of oil production and oil shipments through Latvian ports.

A similar pattern can be seen in the case of Estonia. Russian criticism of Estonia, for instance, largely receded when Gazprom was allowed to participate in Estonia's privatization policies. Lithuania has come in for less criticism because its Russian minority is smaller and better integrated, but economic interests have also influenced Russian policy toward Vilnius. At the end of January 1999, Russia suspended oil deliveries to Lithuania in an apparent attempt to pressure Lithuania into accepting LUKoil's bid for a 33 percent interest in Lithuania's oil sector plus discount tariffs for LUKoil exports via Lithuania. These examples suggest that Russian policy toward the Baltic states is influenced by a variety of factors, not simply concern for the minority issue.

It should be noted, however, that there has been a visible shift in Russian policy toward the Baltic states in the last couple of years. In the initial period after the withdrawal of Russian troops from the Baltic states, Russian policy was often characterized by bluster and sharp criticism of the Baltic states, especially over the minority issue. At the beginning of 1997, for instance, then Foreign

Minister Yevgeni Primakov openly threatened to impose economic sanctions against the Baltic states. Moscow has also dragged its heels regarding the signing of border agreements with Estonia and Latvia and has tried to use the border issue as a means of wresting political concessions over the treatment of the Russian minority, especially from Estonia.

Recently, however, Russia has shown a more pronounced interest in cooperation with the Baltic states. During the meeting of Baltic and Central European states in Vilnius in September 1997, then Prime Minister Viktor Chernomyrdin proposed a series of confidence-building measures designed to ease tensions in the Baltic region. In addition, he called for the Baltic states to adopt a non-bloc status similar to that of Finland and Sweden and said that Russia was ready to offer the Baltic states (and Sweden and Finland) unilateral security guarantees.

President Yeltsin repeated the offer of security guarantees during a meeting with Lithuania's former President Algirdas Brazauskas in Moscow in late October 1997. During his trip to Sweden in December, Yeltsin went a step further, announcing a unilateral 40 percent cut in Russian forces in the Baltic region and calling for the implementation of a series of confidence-building measures similar to those proposed by Chernomyrdin in September. In making the announcement, however, Yeltsin appeared to have been trying to make a virtue out of necessity, since Russia intended to make these cuts anyway, largely for economic reasons.

The Russian proposals represent a mixture of old and new thinking. The main Russian goal seems to be to block Baltic (as well as Swedish and Finnish) membership in NATO and turn the Baltic/Nordic region into a "NATO-free" zone. Such an arrangement, however, is unacceptable to the Baltic states—as well as to Finland and Sweden—because it would effectively foreclose the NATO option and decouple Baltic and Nordic security from European security, leaving the region susceptible to Russia's power and influence.

Although Moscow has not objected to Baltic membership in the EU, it has continued to insist that Baltic membership in NATO is unacceptable and would cross a "red line." How strongly Russia feels about this issue and what it would be willing to do about it is difficult to say. Despite strong objections, Moscow ultimately accepted the first round of NATO enlargement. But Baltic membership in NATO strikes closer to home because the Baltic states border on Russia and were once part of the Soviet Union.

Moreover, Yeltsin's weakened position and the Russian financial crisis add a new sense of uncertainty about the future directions of Russian policy. On the whole, Yeltsin has been a moderating force on Russian foreign policy and a brake on nationalistic tendencies in the Duma. However, the Yeltsin era is rapidly drawing to a close—indeed, many would argue it has already effectively ended—and it is by no means clear that Yeltsin's successor will pursue the same relatively moderate policy, particularly toward the Baltic states. Some prospective presidential candidates, such as Moscow's mayor, Yuri Luzhkov, have consciously sought to exploit nationalism—and the Baltic issue—for their own partisan purposes. Thus, the Baltic issue could resurface as an issue in Russian domestic politics—and in U.S.-Russian relations.

This argues for taking a deliberate, measured approach to Baltic membership in NATO. Russia will need time to adjust to the new strategic realities, and it would be unwise to overload the political agenda. That might spark a destabilizing backlash, which could exacerbate Baltic-Russian relations. At the same time, the United States should reject any effort by Russia to draw "red lines" and should insist that the Baltic states have a right to choose their own security orientation.

In addition, Washington should continue to try to engage Russia—especially northwestern Russia—more deeply in regional cooperation schemes. The more it is involved in these plans, the greater stake Moscow will have in regional stability and the easier it will be to defuse Russian concerns about the security orientation of the Baltic states over the long term.

U.S. Policy Toward Northeastern Europe

KALININGRAD

Kaliningrad complicates the development of an effective U.S. policy toward northeastern Europe. During the Cold War, Kaliningrad—the former German city of Königsberg—was one of the most highly militarized regions in the Soviet Union. The independence of the Baltic states, however, left the Kaliningrad Oblast (region) as an enclave detached from the rest of Russia. The most direct land access to Kaliningrad from Russia is through Lithuania. Many Lithuanians fear that the access issue could be used as a pretext to invade or intimidate Lithuania. Poland, too, is concerned by the high concentration of Russian forces in the region and has pressed for the demilitarization of the oblast.

The region, however, remains strategically important to Russia. With the loss of the Baltic republics, Kaliningrad is Russia's only remaining warm-water port in the Baltic region. Thus, unlike other possessions acquired after World War II, such as the Kuril Islands, there is little chance that Russia would be willing to negotiate the status of the region. Moreover, the population of the region is now almost entirely Russian.

At the same time, the local authorities in Kaliningrad want to exploit the region's geographic proximity to Europe to foster closer economic ties to the West. Some even dream of Kaliningrad becoming a "Russian Hong Kong" some day. However, to achieve these goals Kaliningrad needs Western capital and investment to expand and modernize its antiquated infrastructure and to develop a modern transportation and communication network.

Integrating Kaliningrad into broader regional cooperation arrangements, such as the Northern European Initiative, could help to address these problems and provide a means to attract the necessary Western capital to achieve these ambitious goals. It could also provide an incentive for Russia to continue to demilitarize the region. Together with St. Petersburg, Kaliningrad could become Russia's gateway and window to the West, helping to link it more closely to Europe. Thus, including Kaliningrad and other areas of northwestern Russia in efforts designed to promote greater regional cooperation in the Baltic/Nordic area makes good economic and political sense.

In 1996, Kaliningrad became a Special Economic Zone. However, the central authorities in Moscow have been wary of a significant expansion of Kaliningrad's ties to the West, fearing that this could result in a loss of central control over Kaliningrad and spur separatist tendencies. At the same time, they have been unwilling to provide the region with sufficient economic assistance to deal with its mounting economic and social problems. As a result, Kaliningrad has become a growing center for crime, arms smuggling, and drug activities, and its economic infrastructure has continued to decay. The region also has the highest incidence of AIDS in the Russian Federation.

The financial crisis in Russia has aggravated Kaliningrad's economic plight. Nearly one-quarter of the region's population is unemployed. In September 1998, the mayor of Kaliningrad was forced to declare a state of emergency and appeal for humanitarian assistance from Poland and the Baltic states. At the same time, the crisis has intensified calls to raise the region's status to that of an autonomous republic within the Russian Federation.

Given Moscow's sensitivities about Kaliningrad, it may be better for the United States to maintain a low profile and encourage others, especially the EU and the Nordics, to play the leading role in dealing with Kaliningrad. This is likely to be more acceptable and less threatening to Moscow than if the United States plays a highly visible role in trying to address the Kaliningrad problem. Poland and Lithuania should also be encouraged to continue to play prominent roles.

At the same time, economic assistance should be provided directly to the local entities and NGOs, not channeled through Moscow, where it is often siphoned off and ends up in the hands of corrupt officials. This would help ensure that Western assistance actually reaches the local groups for which it is intended.

U.S. Policy Toward Northeastern Europe

The Clinton administration has developed an ambitious strategy to promote greater stability in northeastern Europe. The Task Force endorses the general thrust of the administration's policy, especially its emphasis on enhancing regional cooperation and encouraging Russian participation in regional cooperative efforts. Such efforts can contribute to enhancing regional stability and integrating Russia into a broader European framework over the long run. At the same time, the Task Force recommends that a number of steps be taken to enhance the viability and effectiveness of the administration's policy.

First, a senior-level State Department official should be appointed with specific responsibility for promoting regional cooperation in northeastern Europe and coordinating policy toward the region. He/she should report directly to the secretary of state. Unless this is done, there is a serious danger that many of the initiatives that have been launched will languish and/or lose bureaucratic momentum.

Second, the administration should put more resources behind its policy. The administration has laid out an ambitious agenda, but many of its goals are unlikely to be achieved unless they are followed up and sufficient resources are devoted to implementing them. In some areas—particularly regional cooperation between the Baltic states and Russia—there are already signs that momentum is beginning to flag. Many projects have not gotten off the ground because of lack of funds. Moreover, it will be difficult to get America's European allies, especially the Nordics, to do more unless the United States is willing to put more resources behind its vision.

Third, the United States should differentiate between the Baltic states based on their performance and should admit them into Euro-Atlantic institutions individually rather than as a group. This would recognize the growing differentiation that is taking place among the Baltic states. At the same time, it would provide an incentive for those not in the "fast lane" to improve their performance and qualifications for membership in these institutions.

Fourth, the next round of NATO enlargement should include one Baltic state provided that state demonstrates the ability to meet the responsibilities of membership. Admitting one Baltic state in the next round would make clear that there are no "red lines" and complement the EU's decision to put Estonia on a fast track for EU membership. Which Baltic state should be invited—and when—will depend on many factors, especially which one is best prepared to meet the responsibilities of membership at the time when NATO decides to enlarge again. At present, Lithuania has made the most progress in preparing for membership. It also has the best relationship with Russia and the smallest and best integrated Russian minority. Its inclusion in NATO is thus likely to be the least problematic for Russia.

Fifth, the administration needs to do more to generate support for its policy in Congress. This is all the more important because the coalition in Congress that supported NATO enlargement in the first round could break up. Many moderate Democrats and moderate Republicans who supported the first round of enlargement are skeptical about the wisdom of an early second round and especially about including the Baltic states. Keeping the old enlargement coalition together will be difficult and will require sustained effort on the part of this administration or the next.

Sixth, the administration needs to develop greater support for its policy among America's NATO allies. Italy, France, Spain, Greece, and Turkey strongly support a "southern" opening in the next round of NATO enlargement. Germany, a key supporter of the inclusion of Central Europe in the first round of enlargement, is far less enthusiastic about the inclusion of the Baltic states. Thus, putting together a new allied coalition for including the Baltic states in NATO will require considerable diplomatic effort and skill on the administration's part.

However, the issue of Baltic membership in NATO needs to be prudently managed and be part of a broader, multifaceted strategy to enhance stability in northeastern Europe. *NATO membership should be an integral element of this strategy, but it should not be the exclusive or central focus of it.* As part of its effort to develop such a broader strategy, the United States should:

- *Use the Partnership for Peace to increase interoperability and help prepare the Baltic states for NATO membership.* PFP provides an important mechanism for enhancing the ability of the Baltic states to operate more effectively with NATO and for helping them prepare for NATO membership. The United States should increase the number of PFP exercises with the Baltic states as well as provide practical assistance of the kind extended to the three newest NATO members (Poland, Hungary, and the Czech Republic) after they received invitations.

- *Encourage the EU to put Latvia and Lithuania on the fast track to EU membership along with Estonia.* This could provide important reassurance to the Baltic states and act as an important deterrent to Russian pressure or intimidation. It would also relieve some of the pressure for membership in NATO. This, in turn, would reduce Russian anxieties and allow the NATO issue to be managed in a less intense atmosphere.

- *Enhance regional cooperation with Russia, including in the military field.* The more Russia is integrated into broader regional cooperation, the less nervous it is likely to be about Baltic membership in NATO over the long run. This is particularly true in the military field. PFP provides an important vehicle for engaging the Russians and for drawing them more closely into regional cooperation.

- *Encourage the Baltic states to integrate their Russian minorities more completely into Baltic political and social life.* The more the Russian minority is integrated into Baltic society, the less of a problem it is likely to be in each state and the less Russia will be able to exploit the minority issue for foreign policy purposes.

- *Encourage the Baltic states to address their past more forthrightly.* NATO is not just a military organization. It is also about values. As part of their effort to demonstrate their commitment to Western values, the Baltic countries need an honest reckoning with their past, including the Holocaust. They have taken the first step in this regard with the establishment of national historical commissions to deal with crimes committed under Nazi and totalitarian rule. However, these commissions need to be more than just formalities. They must address the crimes in a forthright and honest way. This would help to build bridges to various parts of the American political spectrum and would clearly demonstrate that these countries are committed to Western values.

- *Press the Baltic states to implement the OSCE-compliant legislation that was recently passed in Latvia and Estonia and increase funding to help them do it.* Although on paper the laws have been changed, many of the changes have not been fully implemented because of lack of resources. Increased U.S. funding to help the Baltic states provide language training for the Russian minority is particularly important and should be a top priority.

ADDITIONAL RECOMMENDATIONS

In addition, the Task Force makes the following specific recommendations:

Regional Cooperation
- Support for East European Democracy (SEED) money should be increased and refocused to emphasize social integration and to promote regional cooperation programs with Russia. In addition, there needs to be more interaction and consultation between SEED officials dealing with Russia and those dealing with the Baltics.

- The United States should devote more resources to increasing regional cooperation between the Baltic states and Russia in priority areas: crime prevention, education, rule of law, environment, commerce, and energy.

- The United States should encourage greater regional cooperation in northeastern Europe, especially in cooperation with the EU. However, it should reject efforts to decouple Baltic and Nordic security from European security.

Baltic States

- The United States should use Title 8 money to fund more training and research on the Baltic region. A deeper and more thorough knowledge of the region can contribute to the development of more farsighted policies toward the area.

- The mission of the Baltic-American Enterprise Fund (BAEF) should be reoriented and focused more on helping to integrate the Russian minority into the social and political life of the Baltic countries. In particular, it should focus on supporting language training for teachers in the areas populated by the Russian minority.

- The United States should expand and diversify the American engagement in northeastern Europe and the Baltic areas. This engagement should extend beyond the federal government and should involve business, universities, NGOs, and even individual states. In particular the U.S. government can capitalize on the interest of its upper-midwestern states in fostering close cooperation with the Baltic region similar to the cooperation that has developed between the southeastern United States and Germany.

Europe/Nordics

- The United States should encourage the Nordic states to continue their assistance to and trade with the Baltic states, especially Latvia. The Nordics are the Baltic states' natural partners. Moreover, such assistance is likely to raise less suspicion in Moscow than if the United States plays a highly visible role.

- The United States should step up its cooperation with the EU in northeastern Europe. Finland's prime minister, Paavo Lipponen, has called for a "Northern Dimension" for the EU that is designed to promote regional cooperation with Russia in areas such as energy, infrastructure, and ecology. With Finland assuming the EU presidency in July 1999, this is the ideal time to work out an agreement on how the United States and the EU can cooperate more closely in northeastern Europe. In particular, the United States should work closely with Finland to promote closer EU-Russian-U.S. cooperation in northeastern Europe in areas such as drug-traffic control, energy development, and building civil society.

- The United States should encourage the European Union to accelerate the process of integrating the three Baltic states into the EU. This is particularly true in the case of Latvia, which has the largest Russian minority and whose economy is most tightly connected with the Russian economy. If Latvia's performance continues to improve, the United States should encourage the EU to put Latvia on the fast track toward membership, along with Estonia. This would help anchor Latvia more firmly into Euro-Atlantic institutions and reduce its vulnerability. It would also provide a positive signal for Western investment in Latvia.

- Verbal encouragement and rhetoric must be matched by a willingness on the part of the United States to devote more resources to northeastern Europe. If the United States wants the EU to do more, it will have to do more itself. Otherwise the calls for the EU to allocate more resources to northeastern Europe are likely to have little effect.

Security and Defense
- The United States should encourage the Baltic countries to raise their defense spending to the level agreed to by the three newest members—Poland, Hungary, and the Czech Republic (2 percent of gross domestic product).

- The United States should increase foreign military financing (FMF) support to help the Baltic states implement the plans and priorities identified in the Defense Department study on the military capabilities of the Baltic states ("Kievenaar Study"). The Baltic states should be given preferential treatment because, unlike the other East European states, they had to create their militaries from scratch. This would require only a small increase in resources, but it could be very cost-effective.

- The United States should increase bilateral military cooperation, training, and exercises with the Baltic states within the framework of PFP, as well as provide practical assistance to the Baltic states of the kind that was extended to Poland, Hungary, and the Czech Republic after they received invitations to join NATO.

- The United States should work to the extent possible to defuse Russian security concerns by encouraging greater regional cooperation between Russia and the Baltic states. However, Russia should not be given a veto over the Alliance's decision-making or over the right of the Baltic states to choose their own security orientation.

Russia

- Together with its European allies, the United States should press Russia to renounce officially the fiction that the Baltic states were incorporated "voluntarily" into the Soviet Union in 1940. Such a renunciation would greatly contribute to the normalization and development of Russian-Baltic relations over the long run.

- The United States should encourage Russia to sign the border agreements concluded with Estonia and Latvia.

- The social and economic problems of Kaliningrad, stemming from its physical separation from Russia, should be accorded a higher priority in U.S. policy. However, given Russian sensitivities, the United States should encourage others, especially the EU and the Nordics, to play the leading role. Poland and

Lithuania should be encouraged to continue to address Kaliningrad's mounting economic problems.

- To the extent possible, U.S. economic assistance should be channeled directly to the regions in northwestern Russia rather than going through Moscow. This would ensure that the assistance actually goes to local entities and NGOs rather than into the pockets of the central authorities.

- More U.S. assistance should be directed toward improving Russian-Baltic regional cooperation. At present, the bulk of U.S. assistance is directed toward nuclear-waste management in the Kola Peninsula rather than to promoting Russian-Baltic regional cooperation.

- The United States should use the PFP to engage the Russians in the Baltic region. PFP provides an important vehicle for engaging the Russians and drawing them into closer regional cooperation. This can help to reduce Russia's sense of isolation and diminish its fears over the long term that this cooperation is directed against Russian security interests.

- The United States should encourage the Baltic states to continue to interact with Russia and not turn their backs on Moscow despite the economic crisis. Russia's integration into a regional framework can have important benefits for regional stability over the long run.

ADDITIONAL AND DISSENTING VIEWS

ADDITIONAL VIEW

We agree with the general thrust of the report's recommendation stating that the next round of enlargement should include one Baltic state provided that it demonstrates the ability to meet the responsibilities of membership. We believe, however, that there are and will be other factors that influence any decisions on NATO enlargement, including to the Baltic states. We do the Baltic states no service if we pretend otherwise. In addition to the ability of aspirants to meet the responsibilities of membership, these factors include successful absorption by NATO of the first three new members; greater clarity within NATO concerning its long-term missions and forces; and judgments about the impact of these decisions on the broader security situation in Europe, including relations with Russia and the effects on those aspirant countries still not invited to membership.

Karen Dawisha
Toby T. Gati
Robert Nurick

DISSENTING VIEWS

The admission of Estonia, Latvia, and Lithuania into NATO should for now not be on the policy agenda. Northeastern Europe, for historical and geographic reasons, offers the Atlantic democracies an unparalleled opportunity to engage Russia in economic, political, and military cooperation. The United States should capitalize on this opportunity to draw Russia into the Atlantic community by engaging the Baltic states, the Nordic states, and Russia collectively in a wide range of multilateral activities.

Charles A. Kupchan

As an ardent supporter of NATO enlargement and the alliance's "open door" policy, I regret that I must dissent from the report's recommendation that NATO should include one Baltic state—probably Lithuania—in its next round of enlargement. Although enlargement in the north is generally advantageous to the alliance, and Lithuania has made significant progress on all of the stated criteria for NATO membership, one must also look at enlargement decisions in terms of their costs and benefits to the alliance.

From this perspective, Lithuanian membership in the near term generates few political or military benefits and entails significant costs for NATO's 19 nations. First, accepting Lithuania's bid to join NATO in the near term will generate increased problems with Russia at a time when the nature of the post-Yeltsin regime is in question. We should not complicate this historic problem in the near term by enlarging NATO in the sensitive Baltic region, nor should we believe that prudent self-restraint is the same thing as accepting a Russian veto over alliance policy.

Second, Lithuania, the strongest of the Baltic nations, is still extremely weak. Less than three-tenths of 1 percent of its population is under arms, and its military has no tanks, no attack helicopters, and no fighter aircraft. It has precious little capacity for self-defense and has only immature cooperative-defense relationships with its neighbors. While the Task Force Report correctly notes that for NATO, the Baltic region may be protectable even if it is not defensible, the report suggests no rationale for why the alliance should find it in its interest to accept this burden in the near term.

Third, Lithuania is geographically isolated and sandwiched between Latvia, a candidate for neither EU nor NATO membership, and two nervous nations, Russia and Belarus. Farther out, neutral Finland and Sweden compound the region's security ambiguity, with only Poland providing a direct connection to the alliance. This is not a case of geography dictating destiny, but these facts compound Lithuania's military weakness and magnify the complexities of defense planning in the Baltic region.

Fourth, inviting Lithuania to join NATO in the next round will jeopardize many other recommendations in this study and detract from the Task Force's key ideas on the expansion of regional cooperation, by far its most important contribution.

Finally, pushing Lithuanian membership will also complicate alliance relations and possibly delay the next round of enlargement, which I believe should begin soon after the April 1999 Washington summit.

To improve the likelihood of accession in the mid-to-long term, Lithuania should invest more in defense, continue to work closely with NATO's Partnership for Peace program, widen its cooperative defense activities with its Baltic neighbors and the Nordic neutrals, and deepen its regional cooperation with Russia. Lithuania will one day gain admission to NATO, but timing is critical. Moving too soon on NATO membership for Lithuania will give the alliance a pound of problems in return for only an ounce of additional security.

Joseph J. Collins

TASK FORCE MEMBERS

ANDERS ASLUND is Senior Associate at the Carnegie Endowment for International Peace in Washington, D.C.

IAN J. BRZEZINSKI is Legislative Assistant for National Security Affairs to Senator William V. Roth Jr. (R-Del.).

ARIEL COHEN is Senior Policy Analyst at the Heritage Foundation in Washington, D.C.

JOSEPH J. COLLINS[†] is Senior Fellow in Political-Military Studies at the Center for Strategic and International Studies in Washington, D.C. He is a former U.S. Army Colonel and strategic planner.

KAREN DAWISHA[*] is Professor of Government and Politics at the University of Maryland at College Park, and Associate Director of its Center for the Study of Post-Communist Societies.

PAULA J. DOBRIANSKY is Vice President and Director of the Washington Office of the Council on Foreign Relations. She is also the Council's first George F. Kennan Senior Fellow for Russian and Eurasian Studies. During the Reagan administration, she served as Director of European and Soviet Affairs at the National Security Council.

SHERMAN W. GARNETT is Senior Associate at the Carnegie Endowment for International Peace.

Note: Institutional affiliations are for identification purposes only.
[*]Individual endorses the broad thrust of the report but appends an additional view.
[†]Individual endorses the broad thrust of the report but appends a dissenting view.

TOBY T. GATI[*] is Senior International Adviser at the law firm of Akin, Gump, Strauss, Hauer & Feld in Washington, D.C. She previously served as Assistant Secretary of State for Intelligence and Research and as Senior Director for Russia and the Newly Independent States at the National Security Council.

ROBERT E. HUNTER is Senior Adviser at the RAND Corporation in Washington, D.C., and Vice President of the Atlantic Treaty Association. From 1993 to 1998, he was U.S. Ambassador to NATO.

CHARLES A. KUPCHAN[†] is Senior Fellow at the Council on Foreign Relations and Associate Professor in the School of Foreign Service and Government Department at Georgetown University. He was Director for European Affairs on the National Security Council during the first Clinton administration.

DANIEL F. MCDONALD is President and a Member of the Board of Directors of the Potomac Foundation.

ROBERT NURICK[*] is Senior Political Scientist at the RAND Corporation in Washington, D.C.

MARK PALMER is President of Capital Development Company and Building D.C. LLC. He is former U.S. Ambassador to Hungary and Deputy Assistant Secretary of State for Eastern Europe and the Soviet Union.

PETER W. RODMAN is Director for National Security Programs at the Nixon Center. He has served as Deputy Assistant to the President for National Security Affairs and as Director of the State Department Policy Planning Staff.

DEREK N. SHEARER is Professor of International Affairs at Occidental College and an International Adviser to Ziff Brothers Investments. He served as U.S. Ambassador to Finland from 1994 to 1997.

Task Force Members

W. BRUCE WEINROD is Managing Director and General Counsel at International Technology and Trade Associates in Washington, D.C. He served as Deputy Assistant Secretary of Defense for European and NATO Policy from 1989 until January 1993.

DOV S. ZAKHEIM is Chief Executive Officer of SPC International Corporation, Arlington, Va. He was a Deputy Undersecretary of Defense in the Reagan administration.

Note: Institutional affiliations are for identification purposes only.
*Individual endorses the broad thrust of the report but appends an additional view.
†Individual endorses the broad thrust of the report but appends a dissenting view.

TASK FORCE OBSERVERS

GEORGE KOLT is National Intelligence Officer for Russia and Eurasia at the National Intelligence Council.

CLIFFORD A. KUPCHAN is Deputy Coordinator for U.S. Assistance to the Newly Independent States at the U.S. Department of State.

DAMIAN LEADER is Country Officer for Estonia, Latvia, and Lithuania at the U.S. Department of State.

RODERICK K. VON LIPSEY is Director for Defense Policy at the National Security Council and a Lieutenant Colonel in the U.S. Marine Corps.

Note: Institutional affiliations are for identification purposes only.

APPENDIXES

REMARKS BY U.S. SECRETARY OF STATE MADELEINE K. ALBRIGHT TO STUDENTS AT VILNIUS UNIVERSITY

July 13, 1997

Vilnius University, Vilnius, Lithuania

Thank you, Dr. Pavilionis. It is a wonderful opportunity for me to be here and I want to thank you for making that possible. As an ex-professor, I am always very happy to appear in university settings. There is no university in the United States that can live up to your longevity, and I salute your university for its 400th anniversary. I have visited here before as a professor and researcher in 1992, so I have seen this beautiful city, and I am delighted to see the renovation because it is symbolic of the renovation of this country and generally for the new post–Cold War world.

I have often said that you do not have to be in the heart of Europe to have Europe in your heart. Nowhere is that more true than in Vilnius, in Riga, and in Tallinn. For so many centuries, the Baltic peoples have looked outward—over the plains and forests of this continent, across the sea, and to the world beyond it. You have epitomized the idea of free commerce as a foundation for political freedom and peace. You are multiethnic nations, shaped by many cultures and traditions. Your finest tradition is your tradition of openness.

That tradition defines the community of values that is Europe at its best. But we must also remember that there exists a less benign pattern in European politics.

One is destructive nationalism—not the love of country that unites people for the common good, but the kind of nationalism that turns pride in us into hatred of them.

A second is old-fashioned geopolitics—the cynical, patronizing kind practiced by great powers that have tried to take a carving knife to Europe, determining the fate of smaller nations and fighting over the spoils.

That was the pattern through much of the twentieth century. We have had to learn the hard way that when you tell small and weak nations to bend to the will of big and powerful nations, that is a recipe for war, not peace.

As you know, my own life has been stamped by these forces. I am who I am and where I am because the ravages of Hitler and Stalin drove my family from our home and shaped the way I look at the world. I was fortunate to have escaped; to my sorrow millions, including many of my relatives, did not.

Perhaps no part of Europe has suffered more from the old pattern of European politics than the Baltic states. You lost your security, your freedom, your independence, your prosperity—everything but your spirit and your spine. With all you have lived through, you know that just being part of Europe is not enough. Our challenge is to build a new and better Europe. That is what I want to talk with you about today—our efforts to realize our vision of promises kept, injustice undone, and an undivided Europe begun.

I want to ask you—the young people of Lithuania—to work with me to realize that vision. Your challenge is to entrench political and economic freedom in your country. It is to uphold the values of tolerance and respect for minority rights that democracy and our values require.

Our challenge is to build a fully integrated Europe that includes every European democracy willing to meet its responsibilities. That goal embraces the Baltic nations. History has taught us that your freedom is our freedom. Europe will not be secure unless we work with you and others to make sure you are secure.

Many institutions will help us achieve these goals, including the EU and the OSCE. But a new NATO is also vital, and this week we took another decisive step in renewing NATO by inviting Poland, Hungary, and the Czech Republic to join.

Our goal is to create a new pattern of politics in Europe. We want to ensure that nations can advance their interests only by cooperating within the community we are building, and respecting the rules we jointly establish. We want to close every avenue to the kind of destructive behavior that has made so much of this century so tragic for you and for so many. In this way, enlargement will benefit every European nation—those that join sooner, later, or not at all.

I know many of you want to ask me when you might join NATO. I have the letter you wrote to President Clinton on this issue. Let me make our position clear. NATO will expand again. And the standards we will apply to you are the same we apply to every aspiring nation. A cardinal principle of the new Europe is the right of every country, large and small, to choose its alliances and associations. No nonmember of NATO will have a veto, and no European democracy will be excluded because of where it sits on the map.

We will not punish you in the future just because you were subjugated in the past. As NATO welcomes new members, the fundamental question is this: Which nations are important to our security, and which nations are willing and able to contribute to our security?

NATO is attractive because it is strong, so enlargement must preserve its strength and the credibility of its commitments. That is why we have set high standards.

NATO membership is not an entitlement. It involves the most profound obligations that any nation can accept. It means assuming responsibility for the security of others, just as others assume responsibility for your security.

That is why simply getting into NATO should not be the ultimate end of any nation's foreign policy. NATO is a means to an end, and we have to be sure that every new member is ready to advance the common endeavors of our alliance.

Let me stress that President Clinton and I have spent at least as much time in recent months thinking about those countries that were not invited to join NATO in Madrid as we have about those that were.

We welcome your aspirations and support your efforts to join NATO, which can take place as you show yourselves willing and able to assume the responsibilities of membership, and as NATO concludes that your inclusion will serve the interests of the Alliance.

You are far closer today to the institutions of our community than you were the last time I was here, in 1992. And thanks to what happened in Madrid, when NATO crossed the line of 1945, you are closer than you were last week. It is important that you not define partial success as failure.

Together, we will do everything we can to ensure that no new lines are drawn across this continent—not between NATO's first new members and the Baltic states, not between the Baltic states and your neighbors to the east. That includes Russia.

We reach out to Russia not to compensate it for enlargement, but because our cooperation serves our most vital interests and yours. We acknowledge that we are dealing with a new Russia that is striving to build a vibrant democracy and that is reaching out to the West even as NATO takes in new members.

We believe the quest for security in Europe is not a zero-sum game, in which central Europe must lose if Russia gains, and Russia must lose if central Europe gains. A democratic Russia that knows the West is responsive to its legitimate security concerns is more likely to become the kind of partner we need than a Russia that feels isolated and rejected.

Yesterday in St. Petersburg, I continued to make the case that no country will be excluded from NATO because of history or geography. But we must also continue to make clear that NATO enlargement is not directed at Russia—and you must help us. This process is not about escaping west, it is about gaining the confidence to look to the East in a spirit of cooperation. The fact is, Russia is changing. You are changing. Europe is changing. Changing for the better. Changing for good.

I have spent much of my life studying and teaching about the politics of Europe, about Sovietology, and about diplomacy on a divided continent. Nothing gives me greater joy than the knowledge that so many of the books on my shelves at home are now totally obsolete because the old Europe of concrete walls and barbed wire is no more.

You helped bring that about. We have so much more work to do together in the future. And I welcome your thoughts about what that future will bring. Thank you very much. And now, I hope we can have a classroom discussion.

QUESTION: You have talked a lot about Europe and NATO expansion. It is clear that some countries are in, some are out. During his visit to Poland, Mr. Clinton said that the century was ending with a new, reliable, and democratic Europe that is at peace. We think it is perhaps too early to talk about an undivided Europe. What is your point of view?

SECRETARY ALBRIGHT: I clearly always agree with my president. Let me say that what President Clinton was talking about was that with Madrid we have begun a process, not ended a process. What happened in Madrid was that the line that was created by the end of the Second World War and a divided Europe down the center has in fact ended, and that the process now must continue.

I think there were two very important aspects to the Madrid declaration. One was the restatement of the fact that NATO must remain a strong and cohesive alliance, and that any new members that come in must be producers and not consumers of security. They must add to the strength of NATO. The second, equally important principle that was established in Madrid was the "open door" policy, that NATO was open to any democratic country that could fulfill its obligations to that very strong alliance. We are at the beginning of a process which will end up with what is everybody's dream, which is an undivided Europe. It is a road that will take a while, but I think we have come, as we come to the end of the twentieth century, to the dream of this entire century—to have an undivided Europe which is peaceful.

QUESTION: You were talking about the strength and cohesiveness of the alliance, and on the other hand we have France and the southern European countries talking about the necessity of granting membership to Romania and Slovenia. So, are there any united criteria for entrance? Could you comment or elaborate in more detail about the prospects for American and European cooperation in NATO?

SECRETARY ALBRIGHT: Let me explain a little bit what the process is about. We have been saying for the last few years as the whole issue of NATO expansion came up that it was very important for the applicant states and those who would be invited to be able to fulfill the requirements of NATO membership, which were to have vibrant functioning democratic systems, to have market economies, to have a military that is under the control of the civilians, and to have a military that is capable of active participation within the NATO alliance itself.

The Partnership for Peace, which was created in 1994, enabled many countries to participate and examine and expand their military participation. It was during a meeting in Madrid, as a discussion unfolded about membership, that it became evident that three countries—Poland, the Czech Republic, and Hungary—in fact, met the various criteria. There was a push by a number of countries for Slovenia and Romania to come in. But as you know, decisions at NATO are made by consensus, and there were a number of countries that believed that those two countries have not achieved all the measures.

For instance, Romania, while it has very well begun on the road to fulfilling those criteria, had basically had a free system only for seven months, whereas Poland, for seven years, and that there needed to be a better track record on all those criteria. The president, when he was in Bucharest, encouraged the Romanians to stay the course. The Slovenians are also a new country and as a result of being a new country have not yet acquired the institutions and mechanisms that we also believed were essential for NATO membership.

So I think that the process itself was a democratic one and one which operated within the NATO guidelines. What we have done now is to establish a series of mechanisms whereby the countries which have not gotten in can still participate through an enhanced Partnership for Peace in which there will be what we are calling "Atlantic" dialogues or "intensified" dialogues whereby each individual country can have a much deeper relationship with the NATO countries on a political level to determine what they could be doing to improve their chances for membership. Now we have created the Euro-Atlantic Partnership Council—by the way, it was quite remarkable to sit in Madrid at the table with so many countries not only from Europe but from Eurasia, where we were talking about common values and common principles.

So a great deal was happening and a great deal more will happen. In terms of the cooperation between Europe and the United States, we do that on a daily basis, not only within NATO but in a variety of institutions. We Americans are of European origin. We know our country originated out of Europe, and our relations with Europe are very strong, and America's commitment to Europe is symbolized by the fact that we still have 100,000 troops in Europe. And we also have very close economic and political ties.

QUESTION: Secretary Albright, you have just been for two days in St. Petersburg, talking with Minister Primakov. The Russian mass media and some politicians have declared that NATO enlargement is the biggest mistake since the Second World War. Was this officially reflected somehow in the negotiations?

SECRETARY ALBRIGHT: From the very beginning of this discussion we have known that the Russians have not liked the idea of NATO enlargement. We have told them that the new NATO is not a threat to the new Russia, and they have in fact stated and restated that they are unhappy with NATO enlargement. We have at the same time believed very strongly, as I have stated in my opening remarks, that it is very important to bring Russia into the European community, because an isolated Russia, we believe, is more threatening than a Russia that is part of the new Europe.

The NATO-Russia Founding Act is a mechanism whereby Russia will be able to be a part of discussions of common concern in Europe, and those are when we have discussions, for instance, about peacekeeping in Bosnia, or when we are going to be talking about new threats to us all, that is, terrorism, or drugs, or environmental problems. Those are the kinds of subjects that will be discussed in this new joint council. So we have brought Russia into the system in a way not to have them isolated. But Russia's statements about not liking an enlarged NATO will never impinge on enlarging NATO because Russia may have a voice, but it will never have a veto, and only the countries which are members of NATO will determine who the new members will be.

QUESTION: Madam Secretary, in talking about the extension of NATO and the Baltic states, I would like to ask you about the extension of NATO and educational reform. There has been discussion in Lithuania that preparation for entrance to NATO requires the introduction of military education into the schools. I would like to hear your opinion about this.

SECRETARY ALBRIGHT: I am not sure I know how this is specifically being discussed here in Lithuania, so I do not want to be involved in an internal debate. But let me just say that, as I said in my remarks, nationalism and patriotism are key to the existence of our countries, but when that kind of nationalism crosses a line where it defines itself by hating other people, then it is not useful at the end of the twentieth century and the twenty-first century. I do think that the educational processes these days, generally in every country, should be doing a lot to teach about what democratic institutions are about, to make clear to people that citizen participation is essential in democratic governments, that democracy is a privilege and not a right, that democracy and freedom must be defended, which is clearly nothing that has to be taught to Lithuanians who have defended it. But I think generally that our educational systems need to embed the values of democracy and good citizenship and good international responsibility.

RECTOR PAVILIONIS: To follow up on this question, I have often asked my students whether they think NATO enlargement would be positive, negative, or neutral for universities.

SECRETARY ALBRIGHT: I have not thought of that, but I cannot imagine that NATO membership would be negative. I think that generally, I would imagine, having any country and its universities more a part of the international community is good because it allows for freedom to have exchanges, to feel that you are able to exist in any country that you are secure. So I do not think that it is neutral, but positive.

QUESTION: All of us know that there has been some lobbying about the new candidates for entrance to NATO, and I would like to know how much influence France or other states had in the selection of candidates for membership. And I would just like to quote two sentences from a study made by two U.S. experts on the subject of NATO enlargement and the Baltic states, written by analysts from the RAND Corporation, Mr. Ronald Asmus and Mr. Nurick. They said that "the Baltic states are unlikely to be included in the first tranche of NATO enlargement for one basic reason: insufficient support for their candidacy. Simply put, they do not have the votes." Do you agree that this was the basic reason for the failure of the Baltics to be invited?

SECRETARY ALBRIGHT: No, I disagree. I have stated what the issue was and that is that there are certain criteria or guidelines that current NATO members have developed about what is needed for full NATO membership. I go back the points I made initially, that being a member of NATO is not a gift that is bestowed on a country because it is a nice country or because it has had a difficult history. It is a solemn responsibility. As you know, according to Article 5 of the Washington Treaty, by joining NATO you take on the responsibility of fighting on behalf of another country as if it were your own. That means that you are to make sure that everybody within the alliance is capable of carrying out that responsibility. It is not just an ordinary club. It is the most powerful military alliance in the history of the world. And the Baltic countries at this stage have embryonic military systems.

In addition to that, it is important to have deeply rooted democratic institutions, and functioning market systems that would allow for interchange and trade in a nonarbitrary way. I think that there is no doubt that the Baltic countries have borne the burden of being part of the Soviet Union for decades, and in time that you all will have the appropriate criteria that will put you on track as serious candidates. But I can assure you that it is not on the basis of votes.

QUESTION: Mrs. Albright, just a few days ago, one of your employees, the American ambassador to Sweden, Mr. Thomas Siebert, clearly announced and declared that NATO expansion will not be complete until the concrete Baltic countries, that is, Latvia, Lithuania, and Estonia, have been accepted. My question is, was the ambassador to Sweden, when he stated that, authorized or instructed?

SECRETARY ALBRIGHT: We have said that the whole NATO expansion process will not be complete until the democracies of Europe will be part of it. He has stated what we have all said in different ways.

QUESTION: If I am correct, you said in Slovenia that this is one of the first countries in the next round of enlargement. Does it mean that there are new queues forming now for accession to NATO?

SECRETARY ALBRIGHT: I think that there clearly was a great deal of support for Romania and Slovenia in Madrid. We have said that they are among the strongest candidates for the second tranche. President Clinton and I have said that in order to be part of that second tranche, they have to stay the course of some of the reforms they have instituted and make sure that they live up to the criteria that I mentioned previously. There are no guarantees, and there will be a review in 1999, and at that stage it will be determined who will be invited in the second tranche.

RECTOR PAVILIONIS: I think there might be many more questions, but alas, the time has run out. Before we leave this Aula, I would like to express my very great gratitude on behalf of the audience, university students, and professors. As you have been here already twice, let us start the symbolic integration into NATO by tying you to this university with this university sash. I hope this will remind you of your visit to our university.

SECRETARY ALBRIGHT: Let me just say how much I have enjoyed meeting with you. Some people here look as though they are my age, but there are many young people here, and as secretary of state of the United States, I consider it a privilege to be able to work to have a world in the 21st century, your world, that will in fact be undivided and free, which we will be able to have you take ahold of and do in the 21st century what we were not able to do in the twentieth. I hope very much that you will engage yourselves in your study of international relations and look at what the threats are that face the 21st century and learn the lessons of the twentieth.

Thank you very, very much.

THE UNITED STATES AND THE BALTIC REGION: REMARKS BY STROBE TALBOTT, U.S. DEPUTY SECRETARY OF STATE

July 8, 1998

U.S.-Baltic Partnership Commission, Riga, Latvia
(as delivered)

President Ulmanis, Foreign Minister Saudargas, Foreign Minister Ilves, Foreign Minister Birkavs, ladies and gentlemen: it is a personal pleasure for me to be here today. It was 12 years ago that I first visited Riga. The year was 1986, and I was part of an American delegation attending a path-breaking, window-opening, indeed door-opening conference held in Jurmala. My fellow visitors and I could sense the vitality, the strength and the promise of the Baltic peoples. We also felt their longing for freedom.

I cannot, however, claim that any of us foresaw where those qualities would lead in a few short years: to independence, to democracy, to integration into a new Europe, and to a multidimensional partnership with the United States.

The principal custodian of that partnership on the American side is President Bill Clinton. He has asked me to convey to you all an expression of his greetings—and a reiteration of his commitment. As he told your own presidents on January 16th in Washington, your American friends are committed to help you as you progress toward—and in due course through—the open doors of the Euro-Atlantic community's evolving and expanding institutions, very much including the new NATO.

It is in the national interest of the United States that you regain your rightful place in the European mainstream. The upheavals of the twentieth century have taught us that when any part of Europe is isolated, repressed, unstable or torn by violence, the peace of the entire Euro-Atlantic Community is at risk.

We learned that lesson the hard way in the twentieth century; we must apply it in the right way in the 21st.

We are already doing so. Over the past six months, the commitments we have made to each other under the Baltic Charter have contributed to the prospects for Estonia, Latvia, and Lithuania as individual, distinct European states and to the prospects for Europe as a whole.

In the realm of politics, we have worked together to consolidate your transition to democracy. The United States is supporting the development of local nongovernmental organizations through the new Baltic-American Partnership Fund, an initiative that my friend and colleague, the deputy administrator of our Agency for International Development, Harriet Babbitt, will be visiting each of your countries to discuss next week. We are also participating in the establishment of a graduate school of law here in Riga that will educate students from around the region.

In addition, we are helping you help yourselves in the field of social integration, particularly in support of legislation that meets the OSCE's recommendations on citizenship. Like the United States, Estonia, Latvia, and Lithuania are multiethnic societies. That fact presents both great opportunities and daunting challenges. The United States has learned from its own hard experience that if some members of the community are excluded from the benefits, opportunities, and responsibilities of citizenship, then the society and the nation as a whole suffer. In the Baltic Charter, all four of our nations have vowed to work toward inclusiveness and reconciliation as watchwords for the future. Each of your governments has taken important steps to translate those ideas into reality. As just one example, in May your presidents jointly launched national commissions to study the periods of the Holocaust and of totalitarian rule in each of your countries. We salute you for that.

Let me now turn to economics, another area in which we've made significant progress together. The bilateral working groups envisioned under the Baltic Charter have begun to identify key areas in which we can promote trade and investment. The American co-chair of that bilateral economic effort is my friend and colleague, Undersecretary of State Stuart Eizenstat, who is heading this way later this week. He will be working with your colleagues on many of these same issues at the Council of Baltic Sea States Ministerial on Small and Medium-Sized Enterprises in Vilnius on Friday, July 10.

Agriculture is a priority as well. The United States was pleased to join the Baltic states this morning in signing a memorandum of understanding that will expand our cooperation in that critical area.

In all of our economic efforts, we are putting a premium on partnership with the private sector. It is therefore fitting that more than 30 senior representatives of Baltic and American businesses are participating in this inaugural meeting of the Partnership Council. I look forward to discussing with them later today ways that we can work together to accelerate what has been called a Baltic Revolution—a tide of economic reform and integration that has made this region one of Europe's most promising.

Finally, a word about security. As in the areas of democratization and economic reform, when you gained your independence seven years ago you faced tremendous challenges in meeting your security needs. To help you surmount those challenges, our Department of Defense last year undertook a study of defense plans and programs headed by one of our most capable senior officers, Major General Buzz Kievenaar. I'm very pleased that Admiral Malone and Colonel Stolberg could represent the general here today.

We are now working with your defense ministries to design long-term strategies to strengthen your self-defense capabilities and your ability to contribute to European security and stability. As part of that larger effort, we have developed a common position on the positive role that confidence-building measures can play in enhancing regional security, and we have initiated consultations on a range of arms control issues as well.

Those are just a few examples of the growing number of initiatives on which we are working together—not just in this region but across the continent.

Let me close with a brief word about one of the countries of the Baltic region that we hope will increasingly participate in various cooperative regional endeavors in all of the areas I've touched upon in my remarks—politics, economics, and security—and in others that also deserve mention, such as preserving the natural environment. That country is Russia, a nation with whom you share a complex and often painful history. If Russia can come to see the Baltic states not as a pathway inward for invading armies, or as a buffer against imaginary enemies, but as a gateway outward, to the new Europe of which it seeks to be an increasingly active part, then everyone will benefit—your countries, mine, Russia itself, and the Euro-Atlantic community as a whole. We will all be safer and more secure.

Achieving that goal—like all the objectives I have touched on here today—will be far from quick or easy.

But that said, the extraordinary record of your young democracies gives us, your American friends, reason for confidence and optimism. This past Saturday, on July 4th, we in the United States celebrated the 222nd anniversary of our own independence. Your countries regained their independence only seven years ago. That means we have a considerable head start on you. That is grounds not for self-congratulation—rather, it is grounds for congratulating you. We are filled with admiration at how much you have accomplished in so short a time, and we are proud to be at your side in a great task of making sure that our common future vindicates the sacrifices—and avoids the mistakes—of the past.

Thank you very much.

A CHARTER OF PARTNERSHIP AMONG THE UNITED STATES OF AMERICA AND THE REPUBLIC OF ESTONIA, REPUBLIC OF LATVIA, AND REPUBLIC OF LITHUANIA

January 16, 1998

Preamble

The United States of America, the Republic of Estonia, the Republic of Latvia, and the Republic of Lithuania, hereinafter referred to as Partners,

Sharing a common vision of a peaceful and increasingly integrated Europe, free of divisions, dedicated to democracy, the rule of law, free markets, and respect for the human rights and fundamental freedoms of all people;

Recognizing the historic opportunity to build a new Europe, in which each state is secure in its internationally recognized borders and respects the independence and territorial integrity of all members of the transatlantic community;

Determined to strengthen their bilateral relations as a contribution to building this new Europe, and to enhance the security of all states through the adaptation and enlargement of European and transatlantic institutions;

Committed to the full development of human potential within just and inclusive societies attentive to the promotion of harmonious and equitable relations among individuals belonging to diverse ethnic and religious groups;

Avowing a common interest in developing cooperative, mutually respectful relations with all other states in the region;

Recalling the friendly relations that have been continuously maintained between the United States of America and the Republic of Estonia, the Republic of Latvia, and the Republic of Lithuania since 1922;

Further recalling that the United States of America never recognized the forcible incorporation of Estonia, Latvia, and Lithuania into the USSR in 1940 but rather regards their statehood as uninterrupted since the establishment of their independence, a policy which the United States has restated continuously for five decades;

Celebrating the rich contributions that immigrants from Estonia, Latvia, and Lithuania have made to the multi-ethnic culture of the United States of America, as well as the European heritage enjoyed by the United States as a beneficiary of the contributions of intellectuals, artists, and Hanseatic traders from the Baltic states to the development of Europe; praising the contributions of U.S. citizens to the liberation and rebuilding of Estonia, Latvia, and Lithuania;

Affirm as a political commitment declared at the highest level, the following principles and procedures to guide their individual and joint efforts to achieve the goals of this Charter.

Principles of Partnership
The United States of America has a real, profound, and enduring interest in the independence, sovereignty, territorial integrity, and security of Estonia, Latvia, and Lithuania.

The United States of America warmly welcomes the success of Estonia, Latvia, and Lithuania in regaining their freedom and resuming their rightful places in the community of nations.

The United States of America respects the sacrifices and hardships undertaken by the people of Estonia, Latvia, and Lithuania to re-establish their independence. It encourages efforts by these states to continue to expand their political, economic, security, and social ties with other nations as full members of the transatlantic community.

The Partners affirm their commitment to the rule of law as a foundation for a transatlantic community of free and democratic nations, and to the responsibility of all just societies to protect and respect the human rights and civil liberties of all individuals residing within their territories.

The Partners underscore their shared commitment to the principles and obligations contained in the United Nations Charter.

The Partners reaffirm their shared commitment to the purposes, principles, and provisions of the Helsinki Final Act and subsequent OSCE documents, including the Charter of Paris and the documents adopted at the Lisbon OSCE Summit.

The Partners will observe in good faith their commitments to promote and respect the standards for human rights embodied in the above-mentioned Organization for Security and Cooperation in Europe (OSCE) documents and in the Universal Declaration on Human Rights. They will implement their legislation protecting such human rights fully and equitably.

The United States of America commends the measures taken by Estonia, Latvia, and Lithuania to advance the integration of Europe by establishing close cooperative relations among themselves and with their neighbors, as well as their promotion of regional cooperation through their participation in fora such as the Baltic Assembly, Baltic Council of Ministers, and the Council of Baltic Sea States.

Viewing good neighborly relations as fundamental to overall security and stability in the transatlantic community, Estonia, Latvia, and Lithuania reaffirm their determination to further enhance bilateral relations between themselves and with other neighboring states.

The Partners will intensify their efforts to promote the security, prosperity, and stability of the region. The Partners will draw on the points noted below in focusing their efforts to deepen the integration of the Baltic states into transatlantic and European institutions, promote cooperation in security and defense, and develop the economies of Estonia, Latvia, and Lithuania.

A Commitment to Integration

As part of a common vision of a Europe whole and free, the Partners declare that their shared goal is the full integration of Estonia, Latvia, and Lithuania into European and transatlantic political, economic, security, and defense institutions. Europe will not be fully secure unless Estonia, Latvia, and Lithuania each are secure.

The Partners reaffirm their commitment to the principle, established in the Helsinki Final Act, repeated in the Budapest and Lisbon OSCE summit declarations, and also contained in the OSCE Code of Conduct on Politico-Military Aspects of Security, that the security of all states in the Euro-Atlantic community is indivisible.

The Partners further share a commitment to the core principle, also articulated in the OSCE Code of Conduct and reiterated in subsequent OSCE summit declarations, that each state has the inherent right to individual and collective self-defense as well as the right freely to choose its own security arrangements, including treaties of alliance.

The Partners support the vital role being played by a number of complementary institutions and bodies—including the OSCE, the European Union (EU), the West European Union (WEU) the North Atlantic Treaty Organization (NATO), the Euro-Atlantic Partnership Council (EAPC), the Council of Europe (COE), and the Council of Baltic Sea States (CBSS)—in achieving the partners' shared goal of an integrated, secure, and undivided Europe.

They believe that, irrespective of factors related to history or geography, such institutions should be open to all European democracies willing and able to shoulder the responsibilities and obligations of membership, as determined by those institutions.

The Partners welcome a strong and vibrant OSCE dedicated to promoting democratic institutions, human rights, and fundamental freedoms. They strongly support the OSCE's role as a mechanism to prevent, manage, and resolve conflicts and crises.

Estonia, Latvia, and Lithuania each reaffirm their goal to become full members of all European and transatlantic institutions, including the European Union and NATO.

The United States of America recalls its long-standing support for the enlargement of the EU, affirming it as a core institution in the new Europe and declaring that a stronger, larger, and outward-looking European Union will further security and prosperity for all of Europe.

The Partners believe that the enlargement of NATO will enhance the security of the United States, Canada, and all the countries in Europe, including those states not immediately invited to membership or not currently interested in membership.

The United States of America welcomes the aspirations and supports the efforts of Estonia, Latvia, and Lithuania to join NATO. It affirms its view that NATO's partners can become members as each aspirant proves itself able and willing to assume the responsibilities and obligations of membership, and as NATO determines that the inclusion of these nations would serve European stability and the strategic interests of the Alliance.

The United States of America reiterates its view that the enlargement of NATO is an on-going process. It looks forward to future enlargements, and remains convinced that not only will NATO's door remain open to new members, but that the first countries invited to membership will not be the last. No non-NATO country has a veto over Alliance decisions. The United States notes the Alliance is prepared to strengthen its consultations with aspirant countries on the full range of issues related to possible NATO membership.

The Partners welcome the results of the Madrid Summit. They support the Alliance's commitment to an open door policy and welcome the Alliance's recognition of the Baltic states as aspiring members of NATO. Estonia, Latvia, and Lithuania pledge to deepen their close relations with the Alliance through the Euro-Atlantic

Partnership Council, the Partnership for Peace, and the intensified dialogue process.

The Partners underscore their interest in Russia's democratic and stable development and support a strengthened NATO-Russia relationship as a core element of their shared vision of a new and peaceful Europe. They welcome the signing of the NATO-Russia Founding Act and the NATO-Ukraine Charter, both of which further improve European security.

Security Cooperation
The Partners will consult together, as well as with other countries, in the event that a Partner perceives that its territorial integrity, independence, or security is threatened or at risk. The Partners will use bilateral and multilateral mechanisms for such consultations.

The United States welcomes and appreciates the contributions that Estonia, Latvia, and Lithuania have already made to European security through the peaceful restoration of independence and their active participation in the Partnership for Peace. The United States also welcomes their contributions to Implementation Force (IFOR), Stabilization Force (SFOR), and other international peacekeeping missions.

Building on the existing cooperation among their respective ministries of defense and armed forces, the United States of America supports the efforts of Estonia, Latvia, and Lithuania to provide for their legitimate defense needs, including development of appropriate and interoperable military forces.

The Partners welcome the establishment of the Baltic Security Assistance Group (BALTSEA) as an effective body for international coordination of security assistance to Estonia's, Latvia's, and Lithuania's defense forces.

The Partners will cooperate further in the development and expansion of defense initiatives such as the Baltic Peacekeeping Battalion (BaltBat), the Baltic Squadron (Baltron), and the Baltic airspace management regime (BaltNet), which provide a tangible demonstration of practical cooperation enhancing the common security of Estonia, Latvia, and Lithuania, and the transatlantic community.

The Partners intend to continue mutually beneficial military cooperation and will maintain regular consultations, using the established Bilateral Working Group on Defense and Military Relations.

Economic Cooperation

The Partners affirm their commitment to free market mechanisms as the best means to meet the material needs of their people.

The United States of America commends the substantial progress its Baltic Partners have made to implement economic reform and development and their transition to free market economies.

Estonia, Latvia, and Lithuania emphasize their intention to deepen their economic integration with Europe and the global economy, based on the principles of free movement of people, goods, capital, and services.

Estonia, Latvia, and Lithuania underscore their commitment to continue market-oriented economic reforms and to express their resolve to achieve full integration into global economic bodies, such as the World Trade Organization (WTO) while creating conditions for smoothly acceding to the European Union.

Noting this objective, the United States of America will work to facilitate the integration of Estonia, Latvia, and Lithuania with the world economy and appropriate international economic organizations, in particular the WTO and the Organization for Economic Cooperation and Development (OECD), on appropriate commercial terms.

The Partners will work individually and together to develop legal and financial conditions in their countries conducive to international investment. Estonia, Latvia, and Lithuania welcome U.S. investment in their economies.

The Partners will continue to strive for mutually advantageous economic relations building on the principles of equality and non-discrimination to create the conditions necessary for such cooperation.

The Partners will commence regular consultations to further cooperation and provide for regular assessment of progress in the areas of economic development, trade, investment, and related fields. These consultations will be chaired at the appropriately high level.

Recognizing that combating international organized crime requires a multilateral effort, the partners agree to cooperate fully in the fight against this threat to the world economy and political stability. Estonia, Latvia, and Lithuania remain committed to developing sound legislation in this field and to enhancing the implementation of this legislation through the strengthening of a fair and well-functioning judicial system.

The U.S.-Baltic Relationship
In all of these spheres of common endeavor, the Partners, building on their shared history of friendship and cooperation, solemnly reaffirm their commitment to a rich and dynamic Baltic-American partnership for the 21st century.

The Partners view their partnership in the areas of political, economic, security, defense, cultural, and environmental affairs as contributing to closer ties between their people and facilitating the full integration of Estonia, Latvia, and Lithuania into European and transatlantic structures.

In order to further strengthen these ties, the Partners will establish a Partnership Commission chaired at the appropriately high level to evaluate common efforts. This Commission will meet once a year or as needed to take stock of the Partnership, assess results of bilateral consultations on economic, military, and other areas, and review progress achieved toward meeting the goals of this Charter.

In order to better reflect changes in the European and transatlantic political and security environment, signing Partners are committed regularly at the highest level to review this agreement.

Other Reports of Independent Task Forces Sponsored by the Council on Foreign Relations

* † *U.S.-Cuban Relations in the 21st Century (1999)*
  Bernard W. Aronson and William D. Rogers, Co-Chairs

* † *The Future of Transatlantic Relations (1999)*
  Robert D. Blackwill, Chairman and Project Director

* † *After the Tests: U.S. Policy Toward India and Pakistan (1998)*
  Richard N. Haass and Morton H. Halperin, Co-Chairs; Cosponsored by the Brookings Institution

* † *Managing Change on the Korean Peninsula (1998)*
  Morton I. Abramowitz and James T. Laney, Co-Chairs; Michael J. Green, Project Director

* † *Promoting U.S. Economic Relations with Africa (1998)*
  Peggy Dulany and Frank Savage, Co-Chairs; Salih Booker, Project Manager

* † *Differentiated Containment: U.S. Policy Toward Iran and Iraq (1997)*
  Zbigniew Brzezinski and Brent Scowcroft, Co-Chairs

† *Russia, Its Neighbors, and an Enlarging NATO (1997)*
  Richard G. Lugar, Chair

* † *Financing America's Leadership: Protecting American Interests and Promoting American Values (1997)*
  Mickey Edwards and Stephen J. Solarz, Co-Chairs

* *Rethinking International Drug Control: New Directions for U.S. Policy (1997)*
  Mathea Falco, Chair

† *A New U.S. Policy Toward India and Pakistan (1997)*
  Richard N. Haass, Chairman; Gideon Rose, Project Director

Arms Control and the U.S.-Russian Relationship: Problems, Prospects, and Prescriptions (1996)
  Robert D. Blackwill, Chairman and Author; Keith W. Dayton, Project Director

† *American National Interests and the United Nations (1996)*
  George Soros, Chairman

† *Making Intelligence Smarter: The Future of U.S. Intelligence (1996)*
  Maurice R. Greenberg, Chairman; Richard N. Haass, Project Director

† *Lessons of the Mexican Peso Crisis (1996)*
  John C. Whitehead, Chairman; Marie-Josée Kravis, Project Director

† *Non-Lethal Technologies: Military Options and Implications (1995)*
  Malcolm H. Wiener, Chairman

---

*Available from Brookings Institution Press ($5.00 per copy). To order, call 1-800-275-1447.
†Available on the Council on Foreign Relations website at www. foreignrelations.org.